*O*ne *of the most tragic aspects of the injustices and atrocities of 1984 is the lack of awareness of the massacre within the current generation and its total absence from Indian history textbooks. This is where Kultar's Mime has played a phenomenal role. Through the medium of art and theatre, it has powerfully displayed the pain and suffering of the victims of the carnage. The efforts of the bright, young and talented creative team are heartening and renew the hope that the future generations will never forget 1984. I had the good fortune of watching the play in Delhi and the sensitivity with which it was presented and the overwhelming response of the members of the public moved me to tears. I express my deepest gratitude to the makers and the actors of Kultar's Mime for bringing the story of the children of the carnage of 1984 to a global platform, for the world to see and to remember.*

HS Phoolka, Senior Advocate, Delhi High Court, Human Rights activist and author

Kultar's Mime is a powerful drama, vividly evoking the experience of violence that beset Sikhs in Delhi following the assassination of Indira Gandhi. The voices of violation connect these events to murderous pogroms the world over.

Dr. Diana Eck, Professor of Comparative Religion and Indian Studies at Harvard University & Director of The Pluralism Project at Harvard

Beyond the trauma and the anger and the grief and the helplessness there is the nagging question of how we can do this to one another. The genocidal action against the Sikhs in 1984, much like that in 2002 against the Muslims in Gujarat, leaves a gaping hole in our identity as a nation. When I saw Kultar's Mime in Chennai it forced me to look again into this hole. And darkness and hopelessness stared back at me. I had thought I would find some artistic closure on 1984 at a personal level with Kaya Taran, my film about 1984, but it continues to elude my grasp. Kultar's Mime doesn't so much lay blame as lay our values of humanity bare. Its gentleness in the face of mindless cruelty is engaging without being enraging in a wistfully compelling manner.
Sashi Kumar, Journalist, founder of Asianet and the Asian College of Journalism; award winning director of the film Kaya Taran

One is used to seeing violence portrayed in theatrical performances — for example in a Shakespearean Play — but the horror of observation in such cases very often is limited by the time which has passed since the events being portrayed took place - which now are 'Ancient History'. Kultar's Mime is free of such masking by the passage of time ... it cannot be set aside or dismissed as fiction. It is all too real. It is all too recent. To be witness to such cruelty - and to be reminded of its repetition in different places and at different times - made me ask myself if one should simply despair. If perhaps our ability to do evil puts humankind beyond redemption? I wonder how many other poems and plays should be being written just now - in order to record and remember those other many cruelties being suffered today by innocents throughout the world. Why then portray such horror if it leads to despair? I have tried to answer my own question thus. We simply cannot let evil win. No matter how hard it is - we must find hope that may allow good to prevail. Was it necessary and appropriate to portray the horrors of the massacre in 1984? Yes it was - because only by acknowledging how low we can fall have we a chance to repent and reform.
Baillie Norman MacLeod, Glasgow City Councilor

Having tracked Delhi 1984 through the prism of law, I am struck by the sheer authenticity of Kultar's Mime even as it takes creative liberties to drive home the enormity of the crime and its human implications. That it was all imagined far away in the US by a young woman, who had been inspired in turn by a poem by her own father, and expressed through actors who are not of Indian origin, makes this artistic achievement all the more remarkable.

Manoj Mitta, Writer, Journalist & Senior editor, The *Times of India* and The *Indian Express*.

Kultar's Mime is a compelling work that examines the trauma- more so than the events- surrounding the tragic 1984 anti-Sikh riots. It does so through the eyes of the most vulnerable of mankind, that of children. The stark and economic nature of the production only underscores the violence and loss experienced by these characters, who tell their stories through a juxtaposition of poetic verse, body movement, and self-narrative. Even in its contemporality, Sarbpreet Singh's use of poetry for telling the story, the actors' emphatic gestures and postures, and the igniting of an intense emotional response in its audiences, all link "Kultar's Mime" with the great dramaturgical traditions of classical India.

Dr. Cecelia Levin, Art Historian

Central to the impact of Kultar's Mime is its simultaneous ability to universalize and particularize the atrocities that humans commit on one another. While many people are familiar with horrors faced by the Jewish community in Europe, the Delhi Pogroms are far less well known outside of the Sikh community. The understanding of organized state violence against Jewish minority communities in Europe develops a familiar context for the audience that helps them to understand the place of 1984 in the history of India and, for that matter, the world. Hence, the process of discovery, horror and empathy that the actors move through as they progress from the familiar to the unfamiliar is mirrored by the audience. Through the play the distant becomes immanent, the unknown becomes known, that which seems foreign becomes personal and real to the audience. Drama, poetry, visual art and music have a profound ability to draw us in, to hold our attention, to engage us in an emotional response, and to leave us asking for more. The power of Kultar's Mime is to move an audience that often knows little of the events of Delhi and India in 1984, to a place of empathy, compassion, knowledge and action.

Dr. Richard Mann, Associate Professor, College of the Humanities, Carleton University

Sarbpreet has remarkably sustained inventive rhyming couplets right through, a literary artifice that aesthetically balances the otherwise horrific butchery that he recounts from eyewitness survivors. Equally, Mehr has dramatized Kultar's Mime so fluently that if we did not know of its origins as poetry, we would have applauded Sarbpreet as a playwright.

Dr. Ananda Lal, The Telegraph, Kolkata; Professor of English, Jadavpur University.

The power and importance of this work is difficult to capture in words, both because it evokes historical atrocities in some sense unspeakable, and because it offers a glimpse of the ineffable healing power of art and faith. In an age when we are besieged on all sides by words and images of violence and injustice fueled by politics and fear, Kultar's Mime offers sorely needed hope. This hope arises from the artistic act of "remembering" in two senses of the word: recalling the past in service to the future, and drawing together members of the human family torn apart by violence. Kultar's Mime is art as witness - witness to deeds we must never forget and witness to a world of justice and peace, a world coming into being.

Alexander Levering Kern, Executive Director, Northeastern University Center for Spirituality, Dialogue, and Service

Kultar's Mime is unusual in that the play employs a framing device of an earlier historical event as a way to explore a more recent one. The production also centrally incorporates visual images of the 1984 massacre of the Sikh community prompted by the assassination of Indira Gandhi. But they are not literal or documentary, they are highly emotive and expressionistic, and in that way can communicate the various stories in a powerful, non-verbal manner. The play is also unusual because is written in free verse. This heightened language has a particular impact; its rhythms present the events in a somewhat ritualistic way and intensify the emotional experience of the audience.

Professor Katherine Mendeloff, University of Michigan, Ann Arbor

Kultar's Mime provides a moving reflection on the pain and horror of the 1984 Pogroms against Sikhs, but does so from the perspective of Jewish art students who reflect upon how best to commemorate the pogrom against Jews in Kishinev 1903. This twist is a brilliant innovation that ties the genocidal violence of 1984 to a broader context of the genocides of others.

The artifice of this play in tying actual testimony accounts within a story of a poem---turned---play is well on the way of finding a poetic and political mode to narrate the horrors of 1984. Within the broader context beyond the Sikh and Jew, this play, through the voiceless mime of the deaf and mute Kultar/Avatar, a synonym of the Jew deadened into the 'Muslim', as well as the dehumanized colonized peoples by European powers, expresses the genocidal story of yet another terrorist nation---state, let loose on a minority for political gain through the means of mobilizing majority nationalistic sentiment. And we must never forget it takes great courage to stand up and bear witness to the crimes that Power commits. Though the testimonial voice may not speak truth as directly as the victims might desire, the political process of seeking justice is impossible without that voice.

Dr. Balbinder Singh Bhogal, Sikh Studies Chair, Hofstra University

This powerful contemplative play bears witness to stories that must be told and shared. It acts as witnesses, as ghosts, as mirrors, and as a stark reminder that our shared collective past is part of our present and future. If we don't learn from our collective past, we may be destined to repeat it. Ignorance does not absolve us of stopping or addressing the injustice suffered by others.

Kathleen Bitetti, artist, curator and co-founder of the Massachusetts Artists Leaders Coalition (MALC)

Thirty years after Sikh carnage, a Boston playwright underscores truths about victimhood and violence. The play characterizes the violence as a pogrom, and not, as the official and media interpretation labels it, a riot. The production also incorporates elements from a long poem that Singh chanced upon last year, about the 1903 pogrom of Jews in Kishinev, capital of Bessarabia, Russia. Hebrew poet Haim Nahman Bialik's In The City Of Slaughter *tells the tale of three days of violence that killed 49 Jews, injured 500, destroyed 1,300 homes and businesses and left 2,000 families homeless. Singh was struck by the similarities of these bloodbaths, 81 years apart. Kishinev too was no spontaneous riot. The bloodshed was preceded by libel, innuendo and propaganda aimed at stoking hatred and fear. The pattern is visible in other incidents too, like the Gujarat massacre of 2002 that Singh writes about elsewhere.*

Beena Sarwar, journalist, artist and filmmaker from Pakistan.

What happens when speech becomes impossible? Is there any way to speak of unspeakable experiences? Kultar's Mime, the first and only theatrical representation of the 1984 massacre of Sikhs in India, provokes these questions. This year, thirty years after the cataclysm, the play is an attempt to give some form to the incoherence of severe pain and loss.

Kultar's Mime is more than a play. It is a jolt, a powerful nudge to the complacency of the Indian state and media. It is a voice of dissent against the state and against silent submission by those inside and outside of the Sikh community. More specifically, the play is a journey into the wounded world of the children of the October-November carnage. The play thaws the frozen experiences of extreme loss and despair of the Sikh community at large. The actors effectively depict the inexpressible pain of muted victims and survivors of 1984 in haunted verse combined with melancholy, melodious music.

Dr. Shruti Devgan, Rutgers University

Kultar's Mime flows back and forth between the present reality of the children and the post-traumatic stress visions of the horrors they experienced …The play conveys in an hour so much crucial information. It reveals "a world in a blade of grass." By becoming very specific about particular stories, the depth of the inhumanity unleashed upon the Sikh community during the Pogroms pierces the audience. The drama of the children humanizes the victims, and reminds us of the depth of darkness that people enact upon each other. It also reminds us that people can and do survive. But the most important thing that Kultar's Mime does is to give a voice to the voiceless. Art is a human way to express and share emotions, and stories, and to bring other people into a particular experience. Kultar's Mime has created visibility around the human tragedy of 1984 with many non-Sikh audiences, building understanding, sympathy and support.

Ek Ong Kaur Khalsa, Sikhnet

Kultar's Mime makes a comparison with the massacre of Jews in the Pogrom of Kishinev in 1903 to widen the social relevance of this play. Interspersed with haunting raga-based melodies, the audience is suspended between a state of disbelief—how could this happen?—and hope—surely, we can learn from this. This play will undoubtedly educate and inform audiences as it travels to India and Canada. The sensitivity with which this historical event is treated here will also urge audiences to remember the atrocities of 1984 while reflecting on the numerous guises in which we allow them to continue unfolding all around the world.

***Dr. Gurminder K. Bhogal**, Associate Professor of Music, Wellesley College*

J Mehr Kaur handled the violence of this production in a clever and tasteful manner, transferring the violent acts to the victim's red headscarf. Whenever the story told of physical or sexual violence, these acts were mimed in relation to the scarf while the victim told his or her story nearby. While I still felt each act deeply, this careful portrayal of violence allowed me to remain physically and emotionally present to hear these important stories....to see such violence live before me, augmented intentionally by the voices, movement, lighting, and music brought me right to the brink of what I was prepared to handle.

Andrea Fife, Utah Theater Bloggers

The most important message that Kultar's Mime conveyed was that we cannot and should not forget and forgive the 1984 Sikh carnage, or for that matter, innumerous genocides that have been perpetrated by the powers-that-be for their selfish interests. Rendered as it is as a dramatized poem, the rhyming but sharp couplets in the play have immense potential to stir the hearts and minds of people with conscience. I congratulate Sarbpreet Singh and Mehr Kaur for taking on this audacious task and proving that there are people "out there" who will listen and take a step towards a better world.

Raghavan Srinivasan, President Lokraj Sanghatan

A deaf and mute boy, helpless and vulnerable, mimed the blood curdling scene of his father's death. The audience listened, a few batting their eyelids to push back burning tears. The play Kultar's Mime by theatre director and college student Mehr Kaur and Sarbpreet Singh, recreated the horror, leaving the wound of the past raw again. The play throws light on the lives of children who were stripped away from their innocent childhood and instead given a burden of sorrows to walk with, the rest of their lives.

Indian Express, Chennai

Kultar's Mime, a dramatized long poem, not only depicts the painful aftermath of the 1984 Sikh carnage, but also brings to the fore the actual facts of the event. The piece, written by Sarbpreet Singh, is immersive theatre combining painting, poetry and music to tell the stories of children who survived the carnage in Delhi.

Sravasti Datta, The Hindu, Bangalore

KULTAR'S MIME

KULTAR'S MIME

Stories of Sikh children who survived the 1984 Delhi massacre

SARBPREET SINGH
AND
J. MEHR KAUR

ISBN: 1523834137
ISBN 13: 9781523834136
Library of Congress Control Number: 2016901843
CreateSpace Independent Publishing Platform
North Charleston, South Carolina

"It cannot be called a riot, it was a massacre...a genocide...1984 is a blot on India's history"

- RAJNATH SINGH, UNION MINISTER OF HOME AFFAIRS, GOVERNMENT OF INDIA, SPEAKING IN DELHI ON DECEMBER 26, 2014

DEDICATION

Kultar's Mime is dedicated to all innocent victims of organized violence who have been targeted because of their identity or their beliefs.

And to these young artists who have breathed life into this tale:

*Will Blanchette, Aidan Connelly,
Evanleigh Davis, Cassandra DeMarco,
Rose Fieschko, Michelle Finston,
Geena Forristall, Sydney Grant,
Ben Gutman, Cody Johnson,
Poornima Kirby, Ross Magnant,
Adelaide Majeski, Allison Matteodo,
Evelyn Oliver, Leah Raczynski,
Catherine Roberts, Christine Scherer,
Ali Weinstein, Addison Willams.*

FOREWORD

Responding to Injustice – A Personal Memoir of Delhi 1984, Uma Chakravarti, Ph.D.

*U*ma *Chakravarti is a feminist historian who taught at Miranda House, University College for Women, Delhi from 1966 to 1998. She writes on Buddhism, early Indian history, the 19th century and on contemporary issues. She is the author of Social Dimensions of Early Buddhism (1987); Rewriting history: The Life and Times of Pandita Ramabai (1998); Gendering Caste Through a Feminist Lens (2002); and Everyday Lives, Everyday Histories: Beyond the Kings and Brahmanas of Ancient India (2006). She has also co-authored Delhi Riots: Three Days in the Life of a Nation (1987); Shadow Lives: Writings on Widowhood (2006); and From Myths to Markets: Essays on Gender (1999).*

Since the 1970s Uma Chakravarti has been associated with the women's movement and the movement for democratic rights and in this capacity she has participated in many fact finding teams to investigate human rights violations, communal riots, and state repression. She was a member of the 'International Tribunal on Justice for Gujarat' in 2002 which reported on the experiences of survivors of the Gujarat riots. In the past as part of women's civil society initiative she has also visited and reported on Kashmir. Her essay 'A Kashmir Diary: Seven Days in an

Armed Paradise' was published in Urvashi Butalia's edited volume, Speaking Peace: Women's Voices from Kashmir (2003).

When news about Indira Gandhi's assassination began to circulate on the morning of 31st October 1984 it was by word of mouth so no one knew what exactly had happened to her till much later in the evening when her death was officially announced on state TV and radio. Until then it was a day like any other. I was at Miranda House, the college for women where I was teaching, with a bunch of students rehearsing for a play that the students were going to take to some inter-college event or other and I was with them because I was the advisor to the dramatic society of our college for that year.

Around 12 noon or so a colleague came and peeped in through the window of the room where we were rehearsing and asked somewhat mysteriously: 'Have you heard the news…?' I said 'No nothing, what do you mean?' but she went off keeping the mystery to herself. This happened on and off through the next two hours; various colleagues would poke their heads in and then leave without us knowing what the mysterious event they were alluding to was. Finally, after the announcement on BBC news came to be circulated the nature of the "event" became clear. Mrs. Gandhi had been assassinated by her security guards. Stunned by the news and confused by the situation we didn't know how to respond. I had a civil rights meeting in the campus, which was held as scheduled and I went to, and I then went home.

We lived as tenants in the house of a Sikh school principal and went straight to Uncle, as we called him and his wife, Aunty Narinder. They lived across from our own door in the corridor and had been like family to us and our two children for the past seven years and we often discussed politics with them. By then they too knew about the assassination so, as we stepped in, Uncle said: 'yeh kya hua?' (what is this that has happened). All of us were deeply concerned with the way Mrs. Gandhi had played politics out in Punjab — first by setting up Bhindranwale against a perfectly justified demand by Punjab for greater autonomy, and then, when she lost control of the situation, by ordering a military operation on the Golden Temple in Amritsar where Bhindranwale was ensconced. This military assault was a deeply offensive act that would leave a permanent scar on the nation. The '*yeh kya hua*' was an acknowledgement that political issues needed to be dealt with politically; assassinations simply replace one set of people in power by others who make the same mistakes, so nothing changes. Instead, things get worse.

The next morning even our middle class neighborhood witnessed the collection of small mobs of people who took over the streets. There were two other Sikh families on our street apart from Uncle and Aunty who were alone in their home as the mobs began to freely roam the streets in the neighborhood. We tried to fend them off and prevent them from attacking the Sikh houses and as we did that I remember being outraged by a 'helpful' student who lived across from our house telling me to change from a salwar-kameez to a sari so that I wouldn't look like a Sikh and would thus be safe. Uncle and Aunty who were more visible because they lived in the front part of the house were persuaded by us to come into our flat at the back so that they would be less visible — it was a poignant moment because until then we had sheltered under their protective care, nurtured by their warmth and affection. Now as Uncle came into our flat he brought in with him his licensed firearm, saying with so much sadness: 'for self-protection'.

We continued to fend off the bunch of mobsters through some mobilization of the neighbors on the streets. Even as we were successful in preventing attacks I was shocked to hear a neighbor say: 'This street is safe because of Uncle and Aunty' who were regarded as decent, implying that if they had not been, the neighborhood would have been attacked. There was petty envy of the other two Sikh families because they were obviously wealthy, and made no effort to hide it from the rest of the neighborhood, composed largely of people with modest incomes. In the evening a police officer who was a friend of Uncle and Aunty's son came and took them away to his colony where they would be safe as no one knew how the next day was going to turn out.

By nightfall there were stories of the water being poisoned by Sikhs. Fortunately, we didn't have a phone so we were insulated from the panic phone calls that many people were exposed to. But next morning was terrible: the papers carried news of attacks and killings on trains of Sikh passengers on the outskirts of Delhi. The emotional exhaustion of the previous day and night culminated in a collapse as I recalled stories of the Partition when I was six and had heard of such killings for the first time. Partition had been traumatic for us as a family though we were never in danger ourselves. We lived across a park from the Bangla Sahib Gurdwara, in Central Delhi, which we often frequented as children.

At that time it was the Muslims who were targets in Delhi and even in that middle class government housing area where we lived we saw strange acts associated with rioting. As my father and I were going to a ration shop to buy our quota of food for the month a group of Hindu and Sikh men came running towards us and told us to go home because there were going to be attacks in the area. My sister and brother actually witnessed a killing of a Muslim man, one among three trying to reach the shelter of a police station; two made it but one was killed before he could get there in time before the attackers got him. My sister has never recovered from that sight. We hid at home, locking ourselves up in fear of what was to come. Soon I had a raging fever of some kind and my mother recalls me crying out in my delirium: why are the Hindus and Muslims killing each other.

Why indeed?

And so, the news of the train killings had literally made me collapse. I slept for 10 hours. Our son locked himself up for a month in a room, speaking to no one, unable to deal with the violence he had witnessed in the city that he had grown up in and loved dearly until then. When my daughter went back to school after 10 days she was outraged to find the school officially mourning for Mrs. Gandhi but not the Sikhs who had died - even she could see the partisan nature of official memorializing.

In the meanwhile, after the curfew was lifted we went to the relief camps that were set up along with a group of people from the PUDR (People's Union for Democratic Rights). Groups of people sat dazed by the events they had witnessed: others angrily described trying to get the police to act and being turned away. This was the beginning of the process that led to the writing of the report entitled "Who Are The Guilty", a report that made a historic intervention in understanding the complicity of the state in the carnage in Delhi.

Before the joint report of the PUDR and People's Union for Civil Liberties (PUCL) was published (within three weeks of the carnage) the report writers received threats of attacks by Congress goons if the report was actually published. Notwithstanding these threats the report was published, and was widely circulated across India, putting the state on the back foot: since then the entire thrust of the state's actions has been to deny its role in engineering the carnage.

Even before the curfew was lifted the first peace marches had happened as concerned citizens took out processions in colonies where hostile crowds of arsonists still had control of the streets.

They went to Trilokpuri, the site of horrifying violence, and found deserted streets with only a few half-crazed souls cowering in fear. Later, Dilip Simeon, a colleague from Delhi University, recalled an event which he has never forgotten, of a child in her mother's arms crying out in fear as she saw a group of people coming towards them: 'meri ma ko mat marna!' (Don't kill my mother!). She thought another attack was imminent — that is what groups of men did to innocent people and I wonder if she has ever been able to get over the fear she experienced in 1984.

We all had such memories. We visited the 'Trans Yamuna' colonies at the periphery of Delhi, where the poor had been relocated during the clean-up of the city, masterminded by Indira Gandhi's son during the Emergency, that had supposedly made them proud possessors of 25 square yard plots, upon which they had built their homes. Some of the worst carnage had occurred in these colonies and we often came across people or stories that would move us in particular ways.

In Garhi in South Delhi I saw a three year old girl who looked mutely at us: she had lost her speech after the attacks in her area killed her father who had been a vegetable vendor. Her face continues to haunt me even today and I do not know if she ever recovered her speech.

Another young woman of about 18 or 19 lost her husband in the at-tacks. She had been married for less than a year and was a few months pregnant in November 1984. The shock had resulted in a miscarriage. This young woman's story made such an impact on me that I went and pleaded with the only Sikh businessman I knew at that time to please-please give her a job so that she could be financially rehabilitated. Though he was sympathetic to her plight he thought I was a bit touched in the head myself: he couldn't give her a job as he ran a truck business, an all-male enterprise if ever there was one. He gave me some money instead for the relief work we were doing.

For years afterwards, and even to this day, I come across stories of 1984. It's like an undercurrent in the life of Delhi. You get into a cab or go to a certain kind of gathering and say 'Where were you when 1984 hap-pened?' and people will tell you their stories — of landing at airports and being hidden, of hair being cut, of getting home to hear more accounts of relatives being killed, of acts of great brutality and occasionally of great generosity.

Perhaps it was these stories and the need to counter the state nar-rative on 1984 that led to my obsession with archiving the voices of the living present. I kept talking about it to everyone until Nandita Haksar, my student from Miranda House and by 1984 a young lawyer, said: 'Okay then let's do it'. She got hold of a couple of tape recorders and a few cassettes, and we formed ourselves into a group of six people who began the process of documenting 1984. It took us three years to collect the narratives, transcribe and translate them, find a publisher, put in money into the publication and then bring the work out (It was published as The Delhi Riots: Three Days in the Life of a Nation).

This book through its narratives picks up on many threads that are woven together in Kultar's Mime being published here for the first time: the terrible killings of innocent families who were mourning for Mrs. Indira Gandhi because they were her supporters — she had given them plots of land that made them independent home owners for the first time. Some were even observing a fast but were mercilessly killed nevertheless. The first narrator in 'The Delhi Riots: Three Days in the Life of a Nation', Nanki Bai, described the rapes of young girls, powerfully portrayed in Kultar's Mime through the unwilling eyes of a child narrator mirroring my memories too of the mute little girl; indeed Kultar could be my mute little girl, in whose mind every horrifying detail of the violence is frozen forever.

The child witness must 'see' the killings and then try to live normally after the bestiality she has witnessed. The mute witness captures the agony of the private hells that the survivors now live in. The mute witness is also a metaphor for the unacknowledged and un-redressed sexual violence that was buried by the complicity of every member of the community and thereafter in every commission of enquiry report. What the broad story line in 'Kultar's Mime' captures marvelously is the 'event' of November 1984 in all its complexity — the bewilderment of those who were attacked and who were actually grieving for Mrs Gandhi, unlike the mobs that went on a killing and raping spree, enjoying their moment of power against those who were actually like them, poor and vulnerable, but without the patrons that the looting mobs had. The genres that Sarbpreet, and Nandita and I had used are very different but they mirror each other in the emotions that have driven us to engage with our past.

Three Days in the Life of a Nation was so voluminous that finally Nandita and I had to leave out some of the interviews that we had conducted, and these missing interviews are now part of my personal archive. It is part of a collection of many other papers; newspaper cuttings, lists of people killed or missing which we had compiled on our visits to the colonies where the worst attacks had taken place. Some photographs, and sundry bits of paper among which only yesterday I found a small piece written by another student Shonali Bose: an account of the play we had created on 1984 which had got lost among my pile of papers.

Shonali is the maker of the film Amu on the 1984 carnage. In 1984 she was a first year student at Miranda House, one among the three or four others rehearsing for their student play when we began to hear the mysterious words, 'Have you heard…' that I have recalled earlier on in this account of 1984. She had her own collection of stories to recount: of what it was like to be in a women's college, locked behind the iron gates of the institution, supposedly for the safety of the students, but subjected to crazy rumors inside those locked gates about students from the Khalsa College, a Sikh institution across the road from Miranda House, who were supposedly going to come and attack 'them' (when actually no Sikh man could venture on to the streets at that time!).

Shonali recalls the terrible experience of being cut off from family and friends, and subjected to the incessant paranoia of young women who feared for their own safety when it was others who had been in danger during those days. When we reopened after some semblance of normalcy was restored it was clear that the dramatic society was no longer interested in the silly little comedies that are the staple of college productions that are taken to drama competitions in the university circuit. Instead, the group wanted to dwell on what they had just experienced: they wanted to create a street play and take it around to make a meaningful intervention in understanding what had happened to Delhi over three days of violence that had changed them forever.

And so, we invited an old student, Anuradha Kapur, who was then teaching at the National School of Drama and who had created a couple of amazing street plays for the women's movement in the early 80s, to run a workshop so that we too could create a play on 1984. Over a month of exercises and improvisations we evolved a play that could capture some of the complexities of a dramatic moment of violence that a city like Delhi had never witnessed before. Around 30 students had joined the workshop and two faculty members including me were also part of the group so we were at very different levels of understanding about what had happened in November 1984. Anuradha sensed a challenge in the situation: producing a play that we could take around to the various colleges in Delhi University as well as the city at the end of a month and that could capture the voice of the city that had witnessed large scale burning, looting, killing and dislocation was not going to be easy.

By the time we began the workshop, Anuradha had done her preparations with creativity and thoughtfulness. Once we went past the usual exercises to loosen up the group, and let the energies and creativity flow, she asked us to break into groups of three or four people. She then gave us improvisations to do based on words that she had clearly thought about for a long time: rumor, victimization, manipulation, dislocation, and breaking the rules of the game.

The word "dislocation" inevitably made the connection to the Partition: the sequence one of the groups made up was the enactment of groups of people leaving their homes and moving forward, joined to each other in a line (looking a little like a train) with a little girl at the very end. As the group moves forward looking bewildered and frightened, the little girl breaks off from the group and runs back to what is being left behind. There is panic among the rest of the group until the girl returns, clutching a raggedy doll that symbolizes home to her now being left behind.

The little improvisations that different groups came up with became the different segments of the play and the script just seemed to emerge quite naturally after that. One of the improvisations was around the distortion of national symbols, which was really quite tough to create. Our group came up with a really powerful improvisation. Four girls sit back to back to look like the four lions of the Ashokan capital which is the emblem of the Indian nation. It is inscribed with the words *'satyameva jayate'* (truth alone will triumph) which may be called the motto of the nation after the adoption of the Indian Constitution in 1950. After a while the four lions who have been immobilized in stone begin to move shaking themselves out from their frozen state, stand up as humans and raise their hands in a violent gesture and begin to kill people around them saying, '*hatyameva jayate*' (killing alone will triumph).

It was a chilling reminder of the way the state itself (comprised of the Congress party) had turned on its people and the political message was clear to at least some of the university audiences. The play itself had begun with a game of *kabaddi* which both sides are playing according to the convention but which suddenly turns violent as one side begins to attack the other. This was one of the improvisations for the theme of breaking the rules of the game.

A technique Anuradha used was to never let the play become monodimensional in its emotional pitch. She would cut into sequences in what I thought was a mad move initially. She interspersed scenes of games with acts of killing; looting and fun with *siyappa*, the ritual mourning of widows in Punjab. Or a sequence centered on politicians who evoke laughter with their crudity would be followed by the circulation of rumors, which were absurd and unimaginable, but became sinister like the unleashing of poisonous gas over fields.

The unimaginable had become real after the Union Carbide gas leaks in Bhopal a month after the anti –Sikh carnage and was understood by the audiences as we took the play around. Among the many locations we performed at were: the Delhi School of Economics (modelled after the London School of Economics) which had the most politically savvy students on our campus; the grounds of a historical monument at Nizamuddin, an elite colony that had come up post Partition; Tilak Vihar, the colony that was now home to the widows of 1984; and finally on March 8 outside the Red Fort as part of the International Women's Day rally in 1985. After that it was time to pack up since examinations began in the first week of April. The bonds that had been established in the group however stayed as did the concerns that had generated the play: when Shonali made her first film it was on 1984 and among its cast was another young actress from the group who was Sikh herself.

There were other college productions. Some activists created a play that was so powerfully enacted on stage at the first anniversary of 1984 that the group of widows who had come to participate in the meeting simply got up and left as they could not bear to be reminded of what they had experienced the year before. Our son and his school theatre group, who had until then only made up plays on the vagaries of the education system, produced their own version of the events of 1984. It ended in a most prescient manner: as one of the turbaned victims of a riot is felled by a mob the turban is slowly pulled off and is swiftly replaced with a cap of the kind normally worn by Muslim men.

This is what has happened in India: the victims of targeted violence have simply shifted to another group of people, the Muslims first and then the Christians too. Kultar's Mime which has now been turned into a performance piece, like the many attempts to use theatre to speak to our audiences in the past, has, and must have, other resonances across the world. That is what we who witness such a range of hatreds and violence today must never forget.

Anyone, but anyone can be a victim.

KULTAR'S MIME

A poem by Sarbpreet Singh

1

He's a little Sikh boy; his name's Kultar
Lives in a place they call `Jamuna Paar'
Smiling cherubic face; he looks so cute
You can hardly tell, he's deaf and mute
Just your average child from a poor home
Is on first glance I am wont to say
I see him busy with his friends at play
When the streets of Tilakvihar I roam
What is it here that I hope to find
In these dusty alleys forbidding unkind

2

Little Billoo an elfin nine year old
Plays hide and seek with our hero young
She's full of life boisterous and bold
But sensitive too, quick to be stung
Angad is older than both of them
A street urchin now (he was a gem)
Been two years since he went school
He's into petty theft and plays the fool
Wants to grow up tough be a macho man
Does boast one day people near and far
Will know of Angad Singh of Tilakvihar
Under bluster and bravado, hide he can
But those of you who've heard his screams
Do know for sure of his fearful dreams

3

Sweet Rano so fair is a demure nineteen
Lucky; she lives in her uncle's house
There was a time she was calm and serene
Now she's jumpier than a little mouse
She's a lovely little lady; a trifle sad
(Rumour has it that she might even be mad)
She's always lost in her private thoughts
She winds her way through the rickety cots
Of the local hospital's mental wards
She was finally able to find some work
Soothing chasing demons that lurk
In infant minds ripped into shards
Her body is young; eyes are old and wise
Sudden sound makes them widen in surprise

4

You may well ask; what's all this about
What's so unique 'bout this motley bunch
The deaf mute boy little girl young lout
By now my friends you must have a hunch
A story I have to tell; indeed it's true
Tilakvihar! now you have clue
Clusters of houses little shanty town
In dull shades of grey and dirty brown
Blister in the face of that cruel land
Like many others of its color and kind
Destitution poverty and the daily grind
Rub faces and dreams deep into the sand
Oh and what a story do I have to tell
Burning passion blind hate and sanity's knell

5

But let my thoughts not wander too far
For our story now has just barely begun
Our hero has more friends in Tilakvihar
'bout whom we have to learn more; anon
Bishan Singh too was a hardy young lad
Was good at times, sometimes he was bad
You could see him running from his room
His mother chasing him with a broom
Walked with a jump and a skip and a hop
As he swaggered down the narrow street
As dear friends strangers he would greet
And to chat and joke with all he'd stop
But fate's been too cruel; chance unkind
The once gregarious lad, is blind

6

And young Sukhi; another precocious child
Thrived in the warm glow of love and care
Affectionate obliging sweet tempered mild
Lovely smile would hardest heart ensnare
Father's darling Mother's pet the lucky one
At work and at play like a star she shone
What is that the same girl? It cannot be!
Wicked illusion; what do my eyes see?
Withered shell pale cheeks sunken eyes
No signs of the old spark or even life
What caused all this? What kind of strife?
What changed laughter to heaving sighs
We begin to see that all is not well
Each child in the town has a tale to tell

7

And Kultar plays on in the heat and dust
Unaware of the peeping prying eyes
That want to pierce his innocent crust
And the ears that strain to hear his sighs
Kultar and Biloo are now playing house
Biloo is feeding her famished spouse
Who's had a very long and tiring day
Chopping wood or maybe stacking hay
An amused Angad lolling in the chair
In the shade of filthy corner tea shop
Laps tea from a saucer to the last drop
Towards each passerby shifts his stare
Summer afternoon lazy languorous long
Teashop waiter sings an off colour song

8

Look down the street; what do we see
Dhoti clad man trudges his way home
His back is hunched he's bent of knee
Sweat glistens on his balding dome
On his back he carries a box of soap
From his shoulder falls a heavy rope
Busy with dinner Kultar doesn't look up
He and his wife just play and sup
Sudden movement makes our hero start
And look at the stranger's bent back
The sinuous sinister serpent black
Face pales; fear clutches at his heart
Emotions confused play on his face
The little boy in a trance like daze

9

Gets excited; painful memories stream
His palms tighten on his deaf ears
His lips do part in a soundless scream
His face; it mirrors his darkest fears
The sight of the fibrous twisted snake
Makes him tremble uncontrollably shake
His head explodes he goes back in time
A deathly dance in grotesque mime
He grabs Biloo by the hand and they run
Away from their homes towards the square
Where in times forgotten happier fair
The children would gather; have some fun
And laugh and play in the cooling shade
Of the towering banyan's natural arcade

10

Turns to the tree his shoulders heave
He looks like he's jumping up and down
Each fiber of his body seems to grieve
On his face you can see a puzzled frown
He drags to the tree a most heavy load
Stops at every step to prod it and goad
When it tries to fight him and to resist
He pounds on it with his feet and fist
Stretches his hand for an imagined rope
And fashions from it a hangman's noose
Peers at it closely checks if 'tis loose
Calls mates imaginary to help him cope
With his struggling father as he slips
The noose around his neck and trips

11

Kultar becomes his own father then
His eyes roll around and legs do twitch
His agony my friends beyond our ken
Lifeless body falls into the ditch
Eyes do bulge tongue does protrude
Legs leaden as from granite hewed
And thus does the little boy reprise
His father's violent tragic demise
Angad is here; trembling body lifts
And carries him into the tea shop
Gently lets him in a corner drop
Sprinkled with water; up he sits
Eyes shut tight keep out the fears
Cheeks are wet with salty tears

12

If only he could also shut his mind
Exorcise his demons once and for all
Erase the memories harsh and unkind
That ravage his mind tender and small
How can he forget that fateful day
His head in his mother's lap he lay
Like a thunderclap the news did break
Tears in their eyes hearts did ache
They heard the Widow'd been shot dead
Gray haired Widow with streak of black
Imperious immortal no fear of attack
Her body was cold to the death she bled
Violence she sowed violence she reaped
Thousands like Kultar's parents grieved

13

To them she was dear; Mother they said
The only one who'd ever cared for them
Their goddess fierce, proud nation's head
The only one who, the rot could stem
They cared not about the web she'd spun
With the help of her urbane and 'clean' son
She'd done them good was all they knew
Blind loyalty did their reason skew
She always got their faithful support
Although without the sign of a qualm
She did decree their brethren's harm
And still she got their precious vote
To her they felt they owed a debt
And so they beat their breasts and wept

14

Meanwhile in a different part of town
Far from the slums of Tilakvihar
Flock in homage to the fallen crown
Mourners and idlers from near and far
Canards do fly and rumors are rife
About bloody end to the Widow's life
The crowds get thicker the mobs do swell
Louder and louder sounds her knell
Politicians abound every color and hue
Like vultures drawn to a rotting corpse
The hypocrites pull out the stops
Burst into wrenching sobs anew
Like a virus vile this show of grief
Rages unchecked throughout her fief

15

In Tilakvihar the mourners weep
Scared confused dumbfounded dazed
Much like a frightened herd of sheep
That mills without its shepherd fazed
Know not but of the gathering clouds
That cover the sun like silent shrouds
The storm of vengeance about to burst
With an all-consuming bloody thirst
How can they guess what is to pass
For are they not the faithful ones
Have they not and their wives and sons
Stood by the throne steadfast en masse
The mother's dead what's done is done
They look with hope to her only son

16

Somewhere in the city in a darkened room
The plotters gather and make their plans
They seek to spread mayhem and doom
To begin a surreal murderous dance
Deep piercing eyes; thick tuft on chin
Lyricist of gruesome song of sin
Potbellied thin hair and glasses dark
Face mottled with spots and many a mark
Trade union leader minister to be
Once rabble rouser; political leader now
Before him all the petty criminals bow
Is the last one of the notorious three
From 'up above' their orders have come
To 'teach a lesson' to the arrogant scum

17

Who dared defy and shake a fist
At the power of the glorious crown
They must be made to recant desist
Their heads so proud; they must hang down
What better chance could there ever be
Of a brilliant dazzling victory
The nation's shocked now silent still
Plunder and kill till you've had your fill
Seek out the ones with beards and long hair
Loot their houses and rape their wives
Violate their daughters and take their lives
Cast them all into depths of despair
Teach them the price of raising their head
Pile the streets high with maimed and dead

18

The plans are ready and the trio of doom
With its bloody blueprint in its sights
Emerges in haste from the darkened room
And summons the Party's lesser lights
City councilors and some local thugs
Their favorite trouble making lugs
The Party's goons its salaried sods
Are the leaders of the killer squads
All's ready; groundwork has been done
The leaders are led to a meeting place
Excitement writ on each leering face
Waiting's over; the massacre's begun
It's a golden chance a proving ground
For later favors are sure to abound

19

The city's been divided in several parts
And each one is to a leader assigned
Each group towards its 'borough' starts
To carry out its mission inhuman unkind
Chain of lorries; each group has a fleet
Inside there are stacks and piles so neat
Of iron rods, sticks knives and spears
Crude weapons of death; tridents fierce
Gasoline filled there are piles of cans
That will soon set the whole city alight
Yes it is an awesome and terrible sight
As out towards its goal each convoy fans
But wait everything is not quite set
Foot soldiers are to be recruited yet

20

Columns of death slowly make their way
To the outskirts of the new city slum
Where the Party holds unrivalled sway
On the city's idle felons and scum
Promises are made plunder rape loot
Reprisals they know will be quite moot
Over their heads sits the Party's Hand
Who can touch them throughout the land
Others move to the little shanty towns
'Twere built by the Widow's younger son
Thousands of willing recruits are won
For bloody juggernaut ready to pounce
Of murderous hoodlums there is a slew
Ever eager to join the macabre crew

21

The Party meanwhile is hard at work
Feeding more grist to the rumor mill
Stories are spread of Sikhs who smirk
Distribute sweets and dance their fill
Rejoice openly at the Widow's death
Even as the nation holds its breath
Cunning merchants of death and doom
How cleverly they did fire the loom
Wove a net of falsehood lies and deceit
Apathetic eyes are to misery blind
And are made by canard much more unkind
So the common citizen; man in the street
Is ready to stand by and just look on
As the Party displays its crushing brawn

22

Did it happen I'm tempted to ask
Did men become such brutal beasts
A look at Kultar's face; grey death mask
Brings visions back of devilish feasts
The Party's hordes that are let loose
Unleash terror death mayhem and abuse
The column's dust can be seen from afar
As it thunders down on Tilakvihar
Blood for Blood maddened mobs shout
As from their trucks screaming emerge
And begin their devastating purge
Like a herd of cattle people mill about
As they try to escape the avenging wrath
Of fallen Widow's posthumous bloodbath

23

Door splinters breaks there is a crash
A crowd of men with blood in their eyes
With sticks and swinging clubs do smash
Waste everything that in their path lies
Kultar knows not if he's awake or dreams
Opens his mouth and screams and screams
What a blessing his silent vocal chords
That hide him from the flashing swords
They take his father by his long hair
Beat and kick him as they drag him out
Hurl filthy abuse 'revenge' they shout
Neighbours dazed just stand and stare
His father fights tries to break free
As they drag him to the banyan tree

24

Kultar shakes his head opens his eyes
Looks at Angad's anxious and grim look
Looks at little Biloo as she too cries
As she hugs herself; in her little nook
It's all right now he hears Angad say
Snap out of it chase those dreams away
How can those memories fade or dim
Young eyes do again begin to brim
Once more he sees the hangman's noose
It's slipped around his father's neck
A neighbour at the ringleader's beck
Takes Kultar's father's dusty shoes
The rope is tossed up into the tree
A mighty heave and his feet are free

25

Death doesn't come easy to the old man
He twists and twitches his body shakes
The vile ones yank as hard as they can
They hear a loud snap; his neck breaks
Kultar writhes too on the dirty floor
Soul's in a noose; he can't take more
His mind's a wild animal in a cage
His little body has become a stage
Each and every day the drama of death
Is staged here for the world to see
Come one come all it's all for free
Do not stop now to catch your breath
For it's not over by far; there's more
So many tales; it's hard to keep score

26

All over the city they loot and burn
Plunder pillage rape torture kill
The innocents have nowhere to turn
The mobs haven't yet had their fill
Tilakvihar is just one of the names
The rest of the city too is in flames
Proud community; courage was its fame
Hangs down its head and weeps in shame
The keepers of the law have run amok
Aid the mobs in their dastardly deed
Turn their backs; on those who plead
Arrogantly they taunt and mock
You said you were fighters most brave
As they send them to the smoking grave

27

When I walk the streets of Delhi today
I still see blood mixed with the dust
Each silent stone does seem to say
Scream out aloud you must you must
Relive those terrible days of fear
Faces in the crowd seem to leer
Blood soaked earth it speaks to me
Are you so blind you cannot see
Brothers and sisters I hear you
Don't ever think that we'll forget
Sweet martyrs; we are in your debt
Millions more; they can hear you too
Look in our eyes tears pungent brine
Your resting place to us is a shrine

28

Not warriors nor heroes were you
Just common folk from common stock
You did not ask for the martyrs' brew
That made you different from the flock
You were meek you sought not to lead
You had no wish to suffer or bleed
Was it destiny or a quirk of fate
Exalted you to this hallowed state
To the halls of martyrs did you send
Nameless victims of turbulent times
What did you do commit what crimes
To merit such a violent inhuman end
Whose visions cause my blood to chill
Make even relentless time stand still

29

Yells and the chants are heard afar
Mingled with painful agonized screams
As the pogrom continues in Tilakvihar
Brutality beyond our wildest dreams
Breath in gasps eyes reflect her fears
Down her cheeks stream desperate tears
Four times already the mob has come
Can't shut out its ugly sinister hum
Four times her father and brothers two
Rushed brandishing their shining swords
Four times repulsed the angry hordes
But then more came and the mob grew
To hope for mercy they cannot dare
Their eyes are shut in silent prayer

30

Even louder now is the terrible hum
Once again they pick up their swords
An urgent beat sounds on Death's drum
The river of reason the mob now fords
Launches its final murderous attack
Each man to the wall now has his back
They try to protect the ones they love
What courage what valor, but God above
Even he looks away or has shut his eyes
There are just too many; they do prevail
To pieces is hacked each and every male
The women mute shocked cower like mice
Their peril so urgent acute and so real
Of satanic laughter they can hear a peal

31

She's never been so afraid in her life
She's too young and innocent to comprehend
As they come to her waving stick and knife
She thinks they'll kill her; this is the end
Sweet Rano don't bother to hold your breath
Pray harder yet, but for the boon of death
Don't fear the knife embrace it you must
It's all that lies 'tween you and their lust
You're young and you cannot even think
These are not men but lust crazed beasts
Tonight you're one of their carnal feasts
There are depths where they're yet to sink
They circle around like beasts of prey
Her beautiful face is pallid ashen grey

32

All she can see is a huge circle of hands
Fingers that flex squirm in lecherous glee
Big hands small hands dark hands pale hands
On all of them spots of blood she can see
The lascivious hands and their lewd dance
Realization comes to her in single glance
She begins to tremble and frightfully shake
As a firm hold on her body the hands take
Her body is lifted up high up in the air
By the hands and carried to the next room
Oh desperate day of pain death and doom
She struggles kicks weeps tears at her hair
They toss her roughly on a rickety bed
A resounding blow she feels on her head

33

The hands get to work do their cruel deed
Her innocent body shrinks in utter disgust
The maddened hands pick up terrible speed
To maul the object of their bestial lust
Fearsome feeding frenzy; without a hitch
They tear into shreds each and every stitch
She feels a most violent searing pain
And again and again and again and again
By ravenous mouths the hands are joined
They bite and spit out her flesh and blood
Young innocent body pure and tender bud
Violated and wasted her honor purloined
Sated spent the beasts about her drool
Of raw bubbling flesh her body a pool

34

The women strike up a mournful dirge
As more and more are put to death
Unabated continues the unholy purge
Don't even stop to catch their breath
In the midst of the mob Sukhi sees a face
Familiar from another time and place
For a friendly hand the child does grope
On her face appears a dim ray of hope
She says uncle you're my father's friend
Please save him for he will die for sure
You know him well you shared food and more
How can you cast him off; let his life end
For her trouble she gets a slap on her face
Sends her to the ground in a painful daze

35
Her father lies in the dust supine
They set on him with blows and kicks
His friend shouts loudest kill the swine
And they beat him once more with sticks
The sobbing Sukhi crawls through the band
And takes her father's bloody hand
Looks around and sees a scene from hell
But wait what is this horrible smell
Her father's clothes are suddenly wet
Stream of liquid is poured from a can
A deluge of gasoline covers the man
The terrified child, her father's pet
Sobs turn to screams pitched even higher
As they light a match set him on fire

36
The child still dazed from the hard blow
Refuses to let go of her father's hand
Pain and grief dull her mind she's slow
She gazes blankly fails to understand
Pull the child away she must be mad
We don't kill babies we're not that bad
Hands grasp her and so hard they try
But they cannot infant fingers pry
Father and daughter their bodies merge
They scream in unison writhe in concert
Heart rending sounds of pain and hurt
They kick her scream cajole her urge
But with a grip firm deadlier than death
She hangs on till his very last breath

37

Her little hand; the flames did char
Her eyebrows and her hair are burnt
Her face is the color of coal tar
The crowd's silent; a lesson's learnt
Their heads do now hang down in shame
They thought it was some kind of game
You callous cowards angels of doom
In you too for shame is there room
Smoke from his body will become a ghoul
And haunt you all to the day you die
To corners of the earth you may fly
You can't escape this stench so foul
Her pain will grow thousand fold
In your hearts like cancer take hold

38

May you never have any happy dreams
May you never sleep the peaceful sleep
May you ever wake to sound of screams
May rotting guilt in your souls seep
May the fires keep burning in your mind
May you never see joy or one act kind
May your souls burn forever in hell
May your only music be the knell
May your dreams be scattered to the wind
May your hopes be ground into the dust
May you for forgiveness forever lust
May you lie helpless unmoving pinned
Under the weight of your terrible crimes
Gruesome unrivalled even in these times

39

The trio triumphant roam the streets
Gloating at their successful plan
They marvel applaud the deadly feats
Encourage the mobs whenever they can
The murderers line up to get their fees
A bottle of liquor and a hundred rupees
The union leader like a general proud
Jubilant smiles mingles with the crowd
Few voices of reason are heard to plead
They carry lurid tales of violence seen
To the lackeys of the proud fallen queen
Help them they beg; to death they bleed
Her haughty son does the statement make
When a great tree falls earth does shake

40

Proud inheritor of your mother's throne
Don't forget that we're all mortal men
The seeds of violence that have been sown
Will sprout in each desert hill and glen
They'll flower and when fruit they bear
Cloaks of lies they'll to shreds tear
You don't know what evil you've done
You are the inheritor fortunate son
The tears and sighs of the wounded ones
Will come together in a terrible curse
Will goad you and yours indeed do worse
The widowed wives and the orphaned sons
Each and every day and night they'll pray
A measure of their pain you feel some day

41

Bishan is terrified fears for his life
He cowers in his Hindu neighbour's house
Lajo their neighbour's kindly old wife
Hides him where they keep their cows
The boy peers out through a tiny crack
From there he can see his own home's back
The street is quiet; weird deathly calm
But he's heard stories of horror and harm
His father's fled; mother's all alone
The brave old lady who knows no fear
They won't touch me; I will stay here
So she's left behind to guard the home
They'll keep me safe my hairs so gray
You don't know them; Oh please go away

42

He hears a low most unnatural sound
It's dark he's almost gone to sleep
He jumps to the crack with a bound
Rubs his weary eyes; bends to peep
By the field in which they played games
He can see the towers of mounting flames
By the flickering light what does he see
A crowd of men; a thousand there must be
Danny the Gurkha is in the lead
His khukhri raised high above his head
He hacks at a shape; is it alive or dead
Mob advances at a slow menacing speed
A man with a list in no obvious haste
Points out homes to be laid to waste

43

His eyes are shut he begins to pray
As the mob continues its ominous march
He prays for a miracle; let it go away
But on it comes; it's now by the arch
To the floor in despair does Bishan drop
Behind his house the mob comes to a stop
Despite his fright he has to see more
He raises himself up from the floor
Their little shack has been set alight
It can't be true; he continues to stare
As the drag his old mother by her hair
His heart lurches at her terrible plight
He knows that if he goes out he is dead
Frustrated on the wall he bangs his head

44

Like a bird that's by a snake entranced
He looks again with fear and much dread
His heart is by a burning stake lanced
On her ageing body there isn't a shred
His soul is wracked by shame and pain
On his conscience is a permanent stain
Wants to turn away but is forced to watch
They violate the naked old body; debauch
Till a merciful soul executioner kind
Dagger swoops whistling a mournful note
Rush of blood; slits the woman's throat
A terrible peace falls upon his mind
At her death he grieves but is also glad
They can do no more; her tormentors mad

45

Stupefied dumbfounded he lies on the floor
Soul writhes in agony; he weeps and weeps
A part of him cringes; afraid there's more
Through his being a terrible emotion sweeps
Slowly fearfully the boy opens his eyes
Terrible sight; in anguish out he cries
For as hard he tries with all his might
He can't shut out that terrible sight
Whichever way he turns his head and looks
He sees his mother's ravaged body again
In his eyes he feels a most burning pain
Cruel memory; in him deep has its hooks
The pain in his eyes grows more intense
Of time and place he loses all sense

46

Like the maddened king Oedipus of yore
When he happens to chance upon the truth
The boy's eyes too refuse to see more
Anything to shut out that vision uncouth
His hands rise towards each burning moon
Falls collapses; in a numb dazed swoon
When peace returns Lajo finds him thus
Lying in a pool of his blood and pus
She screams out loud as she sees his face
For where once burned two shining coals
All she can see is a pair of black holes
She shakes the boy right out of his daze
Bishan gets up smiles a smile of peace
The vision has gone; the memory flees

47

Yes these are the children of Tilakvihar
These are their stories of blood and gore
In the corners of Delhi near and far
Go and ask you're sure to hear many more
Each of these children is a living shell
Each day each lives in his private hell
The ones that did all of this roam free
Live under the leafy shade of the tree
That was planted deep by the Party's Hand
How can they touch their faithful dogs
The Party machine's most valuable cogs
Whose writ does run throughout the land
You may plead for justice till you die
There's none to heed your desperate cry

48

Your wounds are your own will never heal
Don't look to them for a soothing balm
They do not can not feel what we feel
No demons in their heads; they're calm
My brothers come here from places far
Lay roses at the shrines of Tilakvihar
Each day remember this gruesome deed
I pray forever may our hearts bleed
Your agony for us is a burning cross
We will gladly bear it upon our back
Our memory will never loosen or slack
You'll shine always in history's dross
We'll never forget your terrible pain
Your martyrdom will not be in vain

Ali Weisntein, Evelyn Oliver, Aidan Connelly, Will Blanchette, Leah Raczynski, Hopkinton High School, June 28, 2013

Michelle Finston, Allison Matteodo, Cat Roberts, Ross Magnant and Christine Scherer, Akshara Theater, New Delhi, October 31, 2014

Michelle Finston, Cat Roberts, Addison Williams and Christine Scherer, The Drum, Birmingham, UK, November 8, 2014

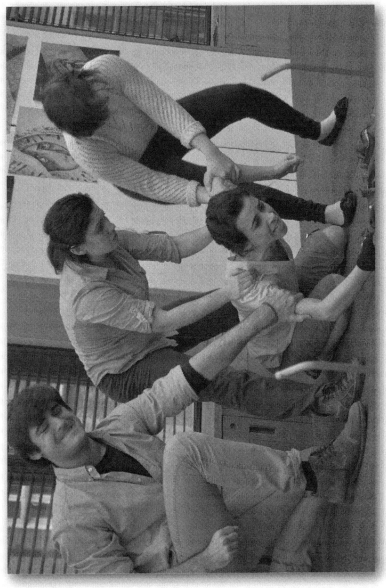

Addison Williams, Michelle Finston, Christine Scherer and Cat Roberts,
British Parliament, Westminster, December 2, 2014

Cat Roberts, Addison Williams, Christine Scherer and Ross Magnant, Portland OR, January 11, 2015

Allison Matteodo, Cat Roberts, Christine Scherer, H.S. Phoolka, Sarbpreet Singh, Ross Magnant, Addison Williams, Adelaide Majeski, Akshara, Delhi, March 22, 2014

Ben Gutman, Sydney Grant, Rose Fieschko, Cassie DeMarco and Ross Magnant, Norman Rothstein Theater, Vancouver, BC, October 2, 2015

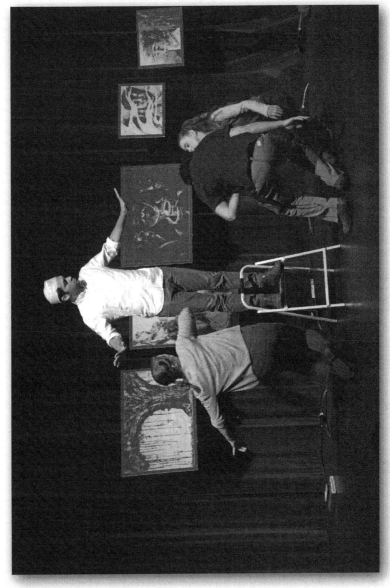

Cassie DeMarco, Ben Gutman, Ross Magnant and Rose Fieschko, Norman Rothstein Theater, Vancouver, BC, October 2, 2015

J Mehr Kaur, Sydney Grant, Ross Magnant, Rose Fieschko, Ben Gutman, Cassie DeMarco, Kings College London, March 12 2015

Ben Gutman, Hofstra University, NY, October 28 2015

KULTAR'S MIME

J. Mehr Kaur
Sarbpreet Singh

Adapted from the poem "Kultar's Mime" by Sarbpreet Singh

*With text from the poem 'In The City Of Slaughter' by Hayim Nahman Bialik
and Var (ballad) 1, Paudi (stanza) 17 by Bhai Gurdas, a sixteenth century Sikh Poet*

CHARACTERS:

There are five characters, four of whom play many different roles.

GUIDE

Advisor to The Applejus Collective, a group of young Jewish artist/activists. Curator of the Kultar's Mime Exhibition

ONE

An artist/activist; plays:
Kultar, a deaf mute Sikh boy
Townsperson
Politician
Party's Hand
Thug

TWO

An artist/activist; plays:
Billoo, a young Sikh girl
Indira Gandhi Shadow
Jagdish Tytler
Thug

THREE

An artist/activist; plays:
Angad, a blind Sikh youth;
Townsperson
Indian Prime Minister Rajiv Gandhi
Lalit Maken
Rano's Father
Thug

FOUR

An artist/activist; plays:

Rano a young Sikh woman

Townsperson

Angad's mother

HKL Bhagat

Thug

[EXHIBITION]

SETTING

The Applejus Collective presents: The Kultar's Mime Exhibition: a traveling art exhibit that makes its way into galleries and site-specific spaces.

GUIDE, the curator of the exhibit leads groups of about ten patrons through the doors of the gallery. She explains that they should feel free to walk around and look at the art before taking their seats for her presentation on the eight pieces created by the collective. She reminds them to silence cellphones, and issues a content warning for sexual and physical violence. She may answer any logistical or seating questions that patrons may have, but asks them to save questions about the artwork itself until the beginning of the presentation.

After the first group has had a chance to look around, GUIDE brings in the second group of patrons, until the whole audience has entered the space.

The artwork is a series of paintings depicting various parts of the story, each of the four children, Indira Gandhi, a mob scene, The Notorious 3 and the banyan tree that figures prominently in the story. The artwork hangs on four 8' by 4' panels, which are plastered with pages from the People's Union for Civil Liberties (PUCL) report on the 1984 Delhi Pogrom. Music is playing in the background.

A recording of an Alap (unmetered elaboration) in Raga Tilang (a North Indian Classical 'scale') is playing in the background.

When all of the patrons have been seated, GUIDE enters the center of the space, to begin her presentation.

[VISIT]

GUIDE

As GUIDE begins her speech, THE ARTISTS appear from a memory. They explore the ruins of Kishinev.

Arise and go now to the city of slaughter;
Into its courtyard wind thy way;

There with thine own hand touch,
And with eyes of thine own head,

Behold on tree, on stone, on fence, on mural clay,
The spattered blood and dried brains of the dead.

Proceed thence to the ruins, the split walls reach,
Where wider the hollow, and greater the breach;

ONE

Pass over the shattered hearth, attain the broken wall

Those burnt and barren brick, whose charred stones reveal
The open mouths of such wounds, that no mending
Shall ever mend, nor healing ever heal.

There will thy feet in feathers sink, and stumble
On wreckage doubly wrecked, scroll heaped on manuscript.

Fragments again fragmented
Pause not upon this havoc; go thy way...

TWO

Unto the attic mount, upon thy feet and hands;

Behold the shadow of death among the shadows stands.

Crushed in their shame, they saw it all;
They did not pluck their eyes out; they
Beat not their brains against the wall!

Perhaps, perhaps, each watcher had it in his heart to pray:
A miracle, O Lord, and spare my skin this day!

THREE

Come, now, and I will bring thee to their lairs

The privies, jakes and pigpens where the heirs
Of Hasmoneans lay, with trembling knees,

Concealed and cowering -the sons of the Maccabees!

The seed of saints, the scions of the lions!

Who, crammed by scores in all the sanctuaries of their shame

So sanctified My name!

FOUR

Beyond the suburbs go, and reach the burial ground.
Let no man see thy going; attain that place alone,

A place of sainted graves and martyr-stone.
Stand on the fresh-turned soil.

There in the dismal corner, there in the shadowy nook,

Multitudinous eyes will look
Upon thee from the somber silence

The spirits of the martyrs are these souls,

Gathered together, at long last,
Beneath these rafters and in these ignoble holes.

GUIDE

See, see, the slaughtered calves, so smitten and so laid;

Is there a price for their death? How shall that price be paid?

Forgive, ye shamed of the earth, yours is a pauper-Lord!
Poor was He during your life, and poorer still of late.

When to my door you come to ask for your reward,
I'll open wide: See, I am fallen from My high estate.

I grieve for you, my children. My heart is sad for you.

Your dead were vainly dead; and neither I nor you
Know why you died or wherefore, for whom, nor by what laws;

Your deaths are without reason; your lives are without cause.

[FIRST CALL TO ACTION]

An abrupt shift to a new memory. THE ARTISTS in a tiny room discussing, deliberating. ONE clutches a Black Book.

THREE

How shall we grieve for the children of Kishinev?

TWO

What is the price to be paid?

THREE

Surely they didn't die in vain?

TWO

Are they forgotten? Does the world remember?

GUIDE

Questions without answers.

ONE

I might have an answer.

ONE holds up the Black Book to the group

TWO

What is this? What kind of answer?

ONE

This Book of Black it burns my hand
This story dark from a distant land
Come hither! Follow! Aloud it screams
Your head I'll fill with fever'd dreams

You will behold a living hell
Discordant chime of desolate bell
Where shattered children drag their feet
Spirits unquiet in each menacing street

Devoid of hope, their eyes are bleak
Not even vengeance do they seek
The memories fade; the bruises pale
As untold withers their bitter tale

ONE shares the Book with THE ARTISTS.

TWO

Are there truly none to calm their fears?
To hear their tales and dry their tears

ONE

Why should we look to someone else?
For is this not our sacred creed?

Why should we not fling out our arms?
To tightly clasp the ones who bleed

GUIDE, who has been reading the Black Book intently, raises her eyes.

GUIDE

Shall we go to Delhi then?

ONE

Seeking justice?

THREE

Or revenge?

TWO

Will we rant? Will we rave?

FOUR

Will we peer in every grave?

GUIDE

We shall do all of that and more.
This hoary tale of gristle and gore.
And yes, before we can be free,
A Kishinev new, we need to see.

THREE

You speak in riddles! A Kishinev new?
There is but one, beneath the sun.
Red with the blood of blameless Jews.

ONE

Oh how I wish your words were true.
But streams of blood. Of many hues.
Flow out of yawning pits of hate.
And when these pitiless floods abate.
Kishinevs sprout in their gory wake.

[STREET SCENE]

The present. GUIDE introduces the paintings. There is music.

GUIDE

Two cities ,
Miles apart ,
No common tongue
No common creed ,
Yet, bound by ties
That hidden lie.

But if you slip off your skin,
And let your spirit float,
Silently ,
Among restless ghosts

A most vexing murmur
You will hear

Anguished cries,
Heaving sighs,
Bitter tears,
Wracking fears

What tongue is this?
You will ask, perturbed

No answer, none,
Your ears will hear

For the spirits speak a language strange
Which is far, far beyond your ken,
It is the tongue of every ghost
Of every maid and every crone
Of every mother and every child

Whose innocent life and smiling eyes,
The savage sword of hate did blight.

Beat.

When I walk the streets of Delhi today
I still see blood mixed with the dust.
Each silent stone does seem to say
Scream out aloud you must you must.

Relive those terrible days of fear
Faces in the crowd seem to leer.

Blood soaked earth it speaks to me
Are you so blind you cannot see?
What is it here that I hope to find
In these dusty alleys forbidding unkind?

KULTAR

He's a little Sikh boy; his name's Kultar.
Lives in a place they call Jamna Paar.
See his smiling, cherubic face? He looks so cute
You can hardly tell he's deaf and mute.

GUIDE

Just your average child from a poor home
Is on first glance I am wont to say.
I see him busy with his friends at play
When the streets of Tilakvihar I roam.

BILLOO

Little Billoo, an elfin nine-year-old
Plays hide-and-seek with our hero young.
She's full of life, boisterous and bold!
But sensitive too; quick to be stung.

Oh Billoo! The little precocious child
Aglow in the warmth of love and care
Obedient loving sweet tempered mild
Her smile would hardest heart ensnare.

Father's darling Mother's pet the precious one
In every way like a star she shone

GUIDE

What! Is that the same girl? It cannot be
Wicked illusion; What do my eyes see ?

Withered shell pale cheeks sunken eyes
No signs of the old spark or even life
What caused all this? What kind of strife?

What changed laughter to heaving sighs?

ANGAD

Angad is older than both of them.
A street urchin now (he was a gem).
It's been two years since he went school.
He's into petty theft and plays the fool.

Wants to grow up tough be a macho man.
Does boast one day people near and far
Will know of Angad Singh of Tilakvihar

GUIDE

Under bluster and bravado, hide he can,
But those of you who've heard his screams
Do know for sure of his fearful dreams.

Yes, Angad Singh was a hardy lad.
Was good at times, sometimes was bad.

You could see him running from his room
His mother chasing him with a broom.

Walked with a jump and a skip and a hop
As he swaggered down the narrow street.
As dear friends, strangers he would greet
And to chat and joke with all he'd stop.

But fate's been too cruel; chance unkind
The once gregarious lad; is blind

RANO

Sweet Rano, so fair, is a demure nineteen
Lucky; she lives in her uncle's house
There was a time she was calm and serene
Now she's jumpier than a little mouse

She's a lovely little lady; a trifle sad
(Rumor has it she might even be mad)

She's always lost in her private thoughts
She winds her way through the rickety cots

Of the local hospital's dingy wards
She was finally able to find some work
Soothing, chasing demons that lurk
In infant minds ripped into shards

ANGAD

Her body is young, eyes are old and wise.
Sudden sound makes them widen in surprise.

GUIDE

You may well ask; what's all this about
What's so unique 'bout this motley bunch
The deaf mute boy, little girl, young lout
By now my friends you must have a hunch

A story we have to tell; indeed it's true

KULTAR

Tilakvihar! Now you have clue.

GUIDE

Clusters of houses, little shanty town
In dull shades of grey and dirty brown
Blister in the face of that cruel land

BILLOO

Like many others of its color and kind

ANGAD

Destitution, poverty, and the daily grind

RANO

Rub faces and dreams deep into the sand

KULTAR

Oh and what a story do we have to tell!

RANO

Burning passion blind hate and sanity's knell

GUIDE

We begin to see that all is not well
Each child in the town has a tale to tell

[THE BANYAN TREE]

GUIDE

Kultar plays on in the heat and dust
Unaware of the peeping prying eyes
That want to pierce his innocent crust
And the ears that strain to hear his sighs
Kultar and Billoo are now playing house
Billoo is feeding her famished spouse

Who's had a very long and tiring day
Chopping wood or maybe stacking hay

ANGAD

An amused Angad lolling in the chair
In the shade of filthy corner tea shop
Laps tea from a saucer to the last drop
To each passerby shifts his sightless stare

RANO

Summer afternoon lazy languorous long
Teashop waiter sings an off color song

GUIDE

Look down the street; what do we see
Dhoti clad man trudges his way home
His back is hunched he's bent of knee
Sweat glistens on his balding dome

On his back he carries a box of soap
From his shoulder swings a heavy rope

KULTAR

Busy with dinner Kultar doesn't look up

BILLOO

He and his wife they play and sup

GUIDE

Sudden movement makes our hero start
And look at the stranger's bent back,
The sinuous sinister serpent black.

KULTAR

Face pales; fear clutches at his heart.
Emotions confused play on his face.
The little boy in a trance like daze.

Gets excited; painful memories stream
His palms tighten on his deaf ears
His lips do part in a soundless scream
His face; it mirrors his darkest fears

The sight of the fibrous twisted snake
Makes him tremble uncontrollably shake

His head explodes he goes back in time
A deathly dance in grotesque mime

GUIDE

He grabs Billoo by the hand and they run
Away from their homes towards the square
Where in times forgotten, happier, fair
The children would gather; have some fun

And laugh and play in the cooling shade
Of the towering banyan's natural arcade

KULTAR

Turns to the tree, his shoulders heave
He looks like he's jumping up and down
Each fiber of his body seems to grieve
On his face you can see a puzzled frown

He drags to the tree a most heavy load
Stops at every step to prod it and goad

When it tries to fight him and to resist
He pounds on it with his feet and fist

Stretches his hand for an imagined rope
And fashions from it a hangman's noose
Peers at it closely, checks if it's loose

Calls mates imaginary to help him cope
With his struggling father as he slips
The noose around his neck and trips

Kultar becomes his own father then
His eyes roll around legs do twitch
His agony my friends beyond our ken
Lifeless body falls into the ditch

Eyes do bulge tongue does protrude
Legs leaden as from granite hewed

And thus does the little boy reprise
His father's violent tragic demise

RANO

Rano is here; trembling body lifts
And carries him into the tea shop
Gently lets him in a corner drop
Sprinkled with water; up he sits

ANGAD

Eyes shut tight keep out the fears

RANO

Cheeks are wet with salty tears

GUIDE

If only he could also shut his mind
Banish his demons once and for all
Erase the memories harsh and unkind
That ravage his mind tender and small
BLACKOUT

[AFTERSHOCKS]

TOWNSPERSON THREE

Like a thunderclap the news did break
Tears in their eyes; their hearts did ache

TOWNSPERSON FOUR

They heard the widow'd been shot dead!

TOWNSPERSON THREE

Gray-haired widow, with streak of black.
Imperious, immortal, no fear of attack.

TOWNSPERSON FOUR

Her body was cold. To the death she bled.

TOWNSPERSON THREE

Violence she sowed, violence she reaped.

INDIRA GANDHI SHADOW

To them she was dear; Mother they said
The only one who'd ever cared for them
Their goddess fierce, proud nation's head
The only one who, the rot could stem

They cared not about the web she'd spun
With the help of her urbane and 'clean' son

She'd done them good was all they knew
Blind loyalty did their reason skew

She always got their faithful support
Although without the sign of a qualm
She did decree their brethren's harm

TOWNSPERSON THREE

And still she got their precious vote

INDIRA GANDHI SHADOW

To her they felt they owed a debt
And so they beat their breasts and wept

GUIDE

Meanwhile in a different part of town
Far from the slums of Tilakvihar
Flock in homage to the fallen crown
Mourners and idlers from near and far

POLITICIAN

Canards do fly and rumors are rife
About the bloody end to the Widow's life

GUIDE

The crowds get thicker the mobs do swell
Louder and louder sounds her knell

Politicians abound every color and hue
Like vultures drawn to a rotting corpse
The hypocrites pull out the stops
Burst into wrenching sobs anew

Like a virus vile this show of grief
Rages unchecked throughout her fief

Beat

In Tilakvihar the mourners weep
Scared confused dumbfounded dazed
Much like a frightened herd of sheep
That mills without its shepherd fazed

TOWNSPERSON FOUR

Know not but of the gathering clouds
That cover the sun like silent shrouds

TOWNSPERSON ONE

The storm of vengeance about to burst
With an all-consuming bloody thirst

TOWNSPERSON TWO

How can they guess what is to pass
For are they not the faithful ones?
Have they not and their wives and sons
Stood by the throne steadfast en-masse?

THE TOWNSPEOPLE address RAJIV GANDHI

RAJIV GANDHI

The mother's dead what's done is done
They look with hope to her only son

BLACKOUT

[THE NOTORIOUS THREE]

Lights up on a darkened room, where the NOTORIOUS 3 are huddled together, plotting.

GUIDE

Somewhere in the city in a darkened room
The plotters gather and make their plans
They seek to spread mayhem and doom
To begin a surreal murderous dance

TYTLER

Deep piercing eyes; thick tuft on chin
Lyricist of gruesome song of sin

HKL

Potbellied thin hair and glasses dark
Face mottled with spots and many a mark

MAKEN

Trade union leader minister to be
Once rabble rouser; political leader now
Before him all the petty criminals bow
Is the last one of the notorious three

GUIDE

From 'up above' their orders have come
To 'teach a lesson' to the arrogant scum

THE NOTORIOUS 3 are showered with paper from the PARTY's HAND.

TYTLER

Who dared defy and shake a fist
At the power of the glorious crown?

HKL

They must be made to recant, desist

MAKEN

Their heads so proud; they must hang down

GUIDE

What better chance could there ever be
Of a brilliant dazzling victory
The nation's shocked now silent still

The NOTORIOUS 3 address the mobs. MAKEN preaches to the crowd.

MAKEN

Plunder and kill till you've had your fill

Seek out the ones with beards and long hair
Loot their houses and rape their wives
Violate their daughters and take their lives
Cast them all into depths of despair

Teach them the price of raising their head
Pile the streets high with maimed and dead

A salute.

GUIDE

The plans are ready and the trio of doom
With its bloody blueprint in its sights
Emerges in haste from the darkened room
And summons the Party's lesser lights

TYTLER

City councilors and some local thugs
Their favorite trouble making lugs

HKL

The Party's goons its salaried sods
Are the leaders of the killer squads

MAKEN

All's ready; groundwork has been done
The leaders are led to a meeting place
Excitement writ on each leering face
Waiting's over; the massacre's begun

GUIDE

It's a golden chance a proving ground
For later favors are sure to abound

MAKEN

The city's been divided in several parts
And each one is to a leader assigned
Each group towards its 'borough' starts
To carry out its mission inhuman unkind

HKL

Of iron rods, sticks knives and spears
Crude weapons of death; tridents fierce

TYTLER

Gasoline filled there are piles of cans
That will soon set the whole city alight
It's an awe inspiring terrible sight
As out towards its goal each convoy fans

MAKEN

But wait everything is not quite set
Foot soldiers are to be recruited yet

Marching.

GUIDE

Columns of death slowly make their way
To the outskirts of the new city slum
Where the Party holds unrivalled sway
On the city's idle felons and scum

Promises are made plunder rape loot
Reprisals they know will be quite moot
Over their heads sits the Party's Hand
Who can touch them throughout the land
Others move to the little shanty towns
'Twere built by the Widow's younger son
Thousands of willing recruits are won
For bloody juggernaut ready to pounce
Of murderous hoodlums there is a slew
Ever eager to join the macabre crew.

[BLOOD FOR BLOOD]

THUG ONE

The Party meanwhile is hard at work
Feeding more grist to the rumor mill
Stories are spread of Sikhs who smirk
Distribute sweets and dance their fill

THUG THREE

Rejoice openly at the Widow's death
Even as the nation holds its breath

THUG TWO

Cunning merchants of death and doom
How cleverly they did fire the loom

THUG FOUR

Wove a net of falsehood lies and deceit
Apathetic eyes are to misery blind
And are made by canard much more unkind

So the common citizen; man in the street
Is ready to stand by and just look on
As the Party displays its crushing brawn

GUIDE

The Party's hordes that are now let loose
Unleash terror death mayhem and abuse

The column's dust can be seen from afar
As it thunders down on Tilakvihar
"Blood for Blood" maddened mobs shout
As from their trucks screaming emerge
And begin their devastating purge
Like a herd of cattle people mill about

As they try to escape the avenging wrath
Of fallen Widow's posthumous bloodbath

[KULTAR]

GUIDE

Did it happen I'm tempted to ask
Did men become such brutal beasts
A look at Kultar's face; grey death mask
Brings visions back of devilish feasts

KULTAR

Door splinters, breaks, there is a crash
A crowd of men with blood in their eyes
With sticks and swinging clubs do smash
Waste everything that in their path lies

Kultar knows not if he's awake or dreams
Opens his mouth and screams and screams

What a blessing his silent vocal chords
That hide him from the flashing swords

BILLOO, ANGAD, RANO, GUIDE

Kultar. Kultar. (in a refrain as the dialogue continues)

KULTAR

They take his father by his long hair
Beat and kick him as they drag him out
Hurl filthy abuse, 'revenge' they shout
Neighbors dazed, just stand and stare

His father fights tries to break free
As they drag him to the banyan tree

BILLOO, ANGAD, RANO, GUIDE

Kultar. Kultar. (in a refrain as the dialogue continues)

KULTAR

Once more he sees the hangman's noose
It's slipped around his father's neck
A neighbor at the ringleader's beck
Takes Kultar's father's dusty shoes
The rope is tossed up into the tree
A mighty heave and his feet are free
Death doesn't come easy to the old man
He twists and twitches his body shakes
The vile ones yank as hard as they can
They hear a loud snap; his neck breaks

GUIDE

Kultar writhes too on the dirty floor
Soul's in a noose; he can't take more

KULTAR

His mind's a wild animal in a cage
His little body has become a stage

BILLOO, ANGAD, RANO

Kultar. Kultar. (in a refrain as the dialogue continues)

GUIDE

Each and every day the drama of death
Is staged here for the world to see
Come one come all it's all for free
Do not stop now to catch your breath
For it's not over by far; there's more
So many tales; it's hard to keep score

THE NOTORIOUS 3 emerge.

MAKEN

All over the city they loot and burn
Plunder pillage rape torture kill
The innocents have nowhere to turn
The mobs haven't yet had their fill

TYTLER

Tilakvihar is just one of the names
The rest of the city too is in flames

HKL

Proud community; courage was its fame
Hangs down its head and weeps in shame

GUIDE

The keepers of the law have run amok
Aid the mobs in their dastardly deed
Turn their backs; on those who plead
Arrogantly they taunt and mock.

[RANO]

RANO is lost in the crowd. The MOB is everywhere.

GUIDE

Yells and chants are heard from afar
Mingled with painful agonized screams
As the pogrom continues in Tilakvihar
Brutality beyond our wildest dreams

RANO

Breath in gasps eyes reflect her fears
Down her cheeks stream desperate tears
Four times already the mob has come
Can't shut out its ugly sinister hum

The Music begins.

GUIDE

Four times her father and brothers too
Rushed brandishing their shining swords
Four times repulsed the angry hordes
But then more came and the mob grew

To hope for mercy they cannot dare
Their eyes are shut in silent prayer

Even louder now is the terrible hum
Once again they pick up their swords
An urgent beat sounds on Death's drum
The river of reason the mob now fords

Launches its final murderous attack
Each man to the wall now has his back

They try to protect the ones they love
What courage what valor, but God above
Even he looks away or has shut his eyes

There are just too many; they do prevail
To pieces is hacked each and every male
The women mute shocked cower like mice

Their peril so urgent acute and so real
Of satanic laughter they can hear a peal

RANO

She's never been so afraid in her life
She's too young and innocent to comprehend
As they come to her waving stick and knife
She thinks they'll kill her; this is the end

RANO'S FATHER

Sweet Rano don't bother to hold your breath
Pray harder yet, but for the boon of death
Don't fear the knife embrace it you must
It's all that lies 'tween you and their lust

You're young and you cannot even think
These are not men but lust crazed beasts
Tonight you're one of their carnal feasts
There are depths where they're yet to sink

THE MOB slinks around RANO in a circle.

RANO

They circle around like beasts of prey
Her beautiful face is pallid ashen grey

All she can see is a huge circle of hands
Fingers that flex squirm in lecherous glee
Big hands small hands dark hands pale hands
On all of them spots of blood she can see

The lascivious hands and their lewd dance
Realization comes to her in single glance

She begins to tremble and frightfully shake
As a firm hold on her body the hands take

Her body is lifted up high up in the air
By the hands and carried to the next room
Oh desperate day of pain death and doom
She struggles kicks weeps tears at her hair

They toss her roughly on a rickety bed
A resounding blow she feels on her head

The hands get to work do their cruel deed
Her innocent body shrinks in utter disgust
The maddened hands pick up terrible speed
To maul the object of their bestial lust

Fearsome feeding frenzy; without a hitch
They tear into shreds each and every stitch

She feels a most violent searing pain
And again and again and again and again

By ravenous mouths the hands are joined
They bite and spit out her flesh and blood
Young innocent body pure and tender bud
Violated and wasted her honor purloined

Sated spent the beasts about her drool
Of raw bubbling flesh her body a pool

[BILLOO]

GUIDE

The women strike up a mournful dirge
As more and more are put to death
Unabated continues the unholy purge
Don't even stop to catch their breath

BILLOO

In the midst of the mob Billoo sees a face
Familiar from another time and place

GUIDE

For a friendly hand the child does grope
On her face appears a dim ray of hope

BILLOO

She says uncle you're my father's friend
Please save him for he will die for sure
You know him well you shared food and more
How can you cast him off; let his life end

GUIDE

For her trouble she gets a slap on her face
Sends her to the ground in a painful daze

BILLOO

Her father lies in the dust supine
They set on him with blows and kicks
His friend shouts loudest kill the swine
And they beat him once more with sticks

The sobbing Billoo crawls through the band
And takes her father's bloody hand

Looks around and sees a scene from hell
But wait what is this horrible smell

Her father's clothes are suddenly wet
Stream of liquid is poured from a can
A deluge of gasoline covers the man

The terrified child, her father's pet

Sobs turn to screams pitched even higher
As they light a match set him on fire

GUIDE

The child still dazed from the hard blow
Refuses to let go of her father's hand
Pain and grief dull her mind she's slow
She gazes blankly fails to understand

THUG ONE

Pull the child away, she must be mad!

THUG THREE

We don't kill babies, we're not that bad.

BILLOO

Hands grasp her and so hard they try
But they cannot infant fingers pry
Father and daughter their bodies merge
They scream in unison writhe in concert

Heart rending sounds of pain and hurt
They kick her scream cajole her urge
But with a grip firm deadlier than death
She hangs on till his very last breath

GUIDE

Her little hand; the flames did char
Her eyebrows and her hair are burnt
Her face is the color of coal tar

The crowd's silent; a lesson's learnt
Their heads do now hang down in shame
They thought it was some kind of game

RAJIV GANDHI perches imperiously above. THE TOWNSPEOPLE and CHILDREN express their anguish and rage.

BILLOO

You callous cowards angels of doom
In you too for shame is there room

Smoke from his body will become a ghoul
And haunt you all to the day you die
To corners of the earth you may fly
You can't escape this stench so foul

Her pain will grow thousand fold
In your hearts like cancer take hold

KULTAR

May you never have any happy dreams
May you never sleep the peaceful sleep
May you ever wake to sound of screams
May rotting guilt in your souls seep

RANO

May the fires keep burning in your mind
May you never see joy or one act kind

BILLOO

May your souls burn forever in hell
May your only music be the knell

KULTAR

May your dreams be scattered to the wind
May your hopes be ground into the dust
May you for forgiveness forever lust
May you lie helpless unmoving pinned

RANO

Under the weight of your terrible crimes
Gruesome unrivalled even in these times

GUIDE

The trio triumphant roam the streets
Gloating at their successful plan
They marvel applaud the deadly feats
Encourage the mobs whenever they can
The murderers line up to get their fees
A bottle of liquor and a hundred rupees
The union leader like a general proud
Jubilant smiles mingles with the crowd

TOWNSPERSON ONE

Few voices of reason are heard to plead
They carry lurid tales of violence seen
To the lackeys of the proud fallen queen
Help them they beg; to death they bleed

THE TOWNSPEOPLE and CHILDREN address RAJIV GANDHI.

TOWNSPERSON FOUR

Proud inheritor of your mother's throne
Forget not you're all mortal men
The seeds of violence that have been sown
Will sprout in each desert hill and glen

TOWNSPERSON ONE

They'll flower and when fruit they bear
Cloaks of lies they'll to shreds tear

TOWNSPERSON TWO

You don't know what evil you've done
You are the inheritor fortunate son

TOWNSPERSON ONE

The tears and sighs of the wounded ones
Will come together in a terrible curse
Will goad you and yours indeed do worse
The widowed wives and the orphaned sons

TOWNSPERSON FOUR

Each and every day and night they'll pray
A measure of their pain you feel some day

GUIDE

Her haughty son does this statement make

RAJIV GANDHI

When a great tree falls earth does shake
BLACKOUT

[ANGAD]

ANGAD

Angad is terrified fears for his life
He cowers in his Hindu neighbor's house
Lajo their neighbor's kindly old wife
Hides him where they keep their cows

The boy peers out through a tiny crack
From there he can see his own home's back

The street is quiet; weird deathly calm
But he's heard stories of horror and harm
His father's fled; mother's all alone

GUIDE

The brave old lady who knows no fear

ANGAD'S MOTHER

They won't touch me; I will stay here

GUIDE

So she's left behind to guard the home

ANGAD'S MOTHER

They'll keep me safe my hairs so gray

GUIDE

You don't know them; Oh please go away

ANGAD

He hears a low most unnatural sound
It's dark he's almost gone to sleep
He jumps to the crack with a bound
Rubs his weary eyes; bends to peep

By the field in which they played games
He can see the towers of mounting flames

By the flickering light what does he see
A crowd of men; a thousand there must be

Danny the Gurkha he's in the lead
His khukri raised above his head
He hacks at a shape; is it alive or dead
Mob advances at a slow menacing speed

A man with a list in no obvious haste
Points out homes to be laid to waste

His eyes are shut he begins to pray
As the mob continues its ominous march
He prays for a miracle; let it go away
But on it comes; it's now by the arch

To the floor in despair does Angad drop
Behind his house the mob comes to a stop

Despite his fright he has to see more
He raises himself up from the floor

Their little shack has been set alight
It can't be true; he continues to stare
As they drag his old mother by her hair
His heart lurches at her terrible plight

He knows that if he goes out he's dead
Frustrated on the wall he bangs his head

Like a bird that's by a snake entranced
He looks again with fear and much dread
His heart is by a burning stake lanced
On her ageing body there isn't a shred

His soul is wracked by shame and pain
On his conscience is a permanent stain
Wants to turn away but is forced to watch
They violate the naked old body; debauch

Till a merciful soul executioner kind
Dagger swoops whistling a mournful note
Rush of blood; slits the woman's throat

A terrible peace falls upon his mind
At her death he grieves but is also glad
They can do no more; her tormentors mad

Stupefied dumbfounded he lies on the floor
Soul writhes in agony; he weeps and weeps

A part of him cringes; afraid there's more
Through his being a terrible emotion sweeps

Slowly fearfully the boy opens his eyes
Terrible sight; in anguish out he cries

For as hard he tries with all his might
He can't shut out that terrible sight

Whichever way he turns his head and looks
He sees his mother's ravaged body again
In his eyes he feels a most burning pain
Cruel memory; in him deep has its hooks

The pain in his eyes grows more intense
Of time and place he loses all sense

Like the maddened king Oedipus of yore
When he happens to chance upon the truth
The boy's eyes too refuse to see more
Anything to shut out that vision uncouth

His hands rise towards each burning moon
Falls collapses; in a numb dazed swoon

GUIDE

When peace returns Lajo finds him thus
Lying in a pool of his blood and pus
She screams out loud as she sees his face

ANGAD

For where once burned two shining coals
All she can see is a pair of black holes

GUIDE

She shakes the boy right out of his daze

ANGAD

Angad gets up smiles a smile of peace
The vision has gone; the memory flees

GUIDE

Yes, these are the children of Tilakvihar.
These are the stories of blood and gore.
In the corners of Delhi, near and far, go and ask.
You're sure to hear many more.

Each of these children is a living shell.
Each day each lives in his private hell.

(ONE, TWO and FOUR walk up to the apron)

BILLOO

The ones that did all of this roam free
Live under the leafy shade of the tree
That was planted deep by the Party's Hand

RANO

How can they touch their faithful dogs
The Party machine's most valuable cogs
Whose writ does run throughout the land

BILLOO

Your wounds are your own, will never heal.
Don't look to them for a soothing balm.
They do not, cannot, feel what we feel.
No demons in their heads; they're calm

KULTAR

You may plead for justice 'till you die.
There's no one to heed your desperate cry.

RANO

Pity me sky.

If a god is within you
and a way to him
I have not found,

pray you for me.

KULTAR

My heart is dead.
My lips mouth no prayer.

Helpless. Hopeless .

How long, how long? How much more?

RANO

Hangman. Here's a throat. Slit it.

Cut my throat like a dog.

You've an arm and an axe
And the whole land for a block.

We are few.
No taboo on my blood.

Crush the skull.
Let the murdered blood
of babes and crones
Spurt on your shirt
and never be blotted out.

BILLOO

If there is justice
let it appear
But if it appear
after annihilation

ANGAD

Let his throne be razed
sky shrivel in evil
devils live in their filth
till their own blood cleanse them.

GUIDE

A curse on the crier for revenge.
Even Satan created no quittance
For a small child's blood.

Let the blood cleave the void
split the bottomless pit
eat away the dark
and rot the foundations
of the putrefying earth.

[REMEMBRANCE]

Having just presented their series of painting, THE ARTISTS remember the children of Tilakvihar.

TWO

Brothers and sisters we hear you
Don't ever think that we'll forget
Sweet martyrs; we are in your debt
Millions more; they can hear you too

FOUR

Look in our eyes tears pungent brine
Your resting place to us is a shrine

ONE

Not warriors nor heroes were you
Just common folk from common stock
You did not ask for the martyrs' brew
That made you different from the flock

TWO

You were meek you sought not to lead
You had no wish to suffer or bleed

FOUR

Was it destiny or a quirk of fate
Exalted you to this hallowed state

TWO

To the halls of martyrs that did send
Nameless victims of turbulent times
What did you do commit what crimes
To merit such a violent inhuman end

TWO, FOUR,ONE

Whose visions cause our blood to chill
Make even relentless time stand still

GUIDE

My friends we come from places afar
To lay roses at the shrines of Tilakvihar
Each day we think of this gruesome deed
Forever, forever our hearts will bleed

THREE

Your agony for us is a burning cross
We will gladly bear it upon our back
Our memory will never loosen or slack
You'll shine always in history's dross

We'll never forget your terrible pain
Your suffering will not be in vain

ONE

Off kilter turns the Wheel of Time and thus do men behave
Anger rules oppression thrives and corruption grave

TWO

Every one is The Other now; of hate an all-consuming fire
Darkness dense is all around; as wisdom's cast 'pon the pyre

THREE

The Holy Books, their precious words; lost in a storm of spite

FOUR

He will set foot on earth again everywhere will be light

GUIDE

Gentle again, the wheel will turn and evil will take flight
Into a million blazing suns shattered will be the night

ALL

Into a million blazing suns shattered will be the night

[END OF PLAY]

TELLING THE TALE 30 YEARS LATER:
THE EXTRAORDINARY JOURNEY OF KULTAR'S MIME

Sarbpreet Singh

TELLING THE TALE 30 YEARS LATER:
THE EXTRAORDINARY JOURNEY OF KULTAR'S
MIME PART 1

On December 26, 2014, Rajnath Singh, the Indian Home Minister, the second most powerful political leader in the new Indian government, dropped a quiet bombshell during a visit to Tilakvihar in Delhi. For the first time in thirty years, an Indian political leader acknowledged that the events following the assassination of then Prime Minister Indira Gandhi were not a 'riot' but genocide!

A scant two months earlier I remember walking up to the immigration counters at Delhi airport, six young American actors from Boston in tow, with more than a little trepidation, unsure of the reception we were going to get in India. For we were in Delhi to present a play called Kultar's Mime. A play that challenged the Goebbelsian notion that the carefully planned massacre of the Sikhs in Delhi in 1984 could be palmed off as a riot!

My immediate family, my friends and my well-wishers had expressed their concern multiple times. Strange things are known to happen even in modern day India to people who have the temerity to offend the powerful. I did not think that we would be harmed in any way; after all we were all US citizens an our first stop was the capital of the country, but it was certainly possible that we would be stopped from performing, which would have been heartbreaking not just for me and my co-director and playwright J Mehr Kaur, but also for the six young actors, who by then were completely invested in the project and had delivered seven rousing performances in the US and Canada before traveling with me to India.

Of course it seemed like a provocative thing to do! To take a crew of young actors, none of them Indian or even South Asian, to the very city where the massacre had occurred, where many of the perpetrators still menacingly stalked the corridors of power and influence, to present a production that unflinchingly portrayed the terrible events of 1984. The plan to perform in Delhi on the exact thirty year anniversary of the massacre was absolutely designed to send a message to the city that had chosen to forget this ugly chapter in its history.

I was outwardly calm as the evening of October 30th, 2014 approached. The set was ready and the actors were done with their warmups. My cheerful exterior hid all kinds of anxieties. Would the police show up mid-performance and ask the audience to leave? Even though the Congress Party was now out of power, would its lumpen elements overrun the small theater, chagrined by the content of the play, which pulled no punches in squarely laying responsibility for the carnage at the Party's door? Would we be declared persona-non-grata and be hustled to the airport that bore Indira Gandhi's name to begin our journey back home with our tails between our legs?

The doors opened and the eager audience streamed in. Members of Parliament and senior diplomats. Powerful bureaucrats, both retired and serving. Artists and students. And to my joy, some of my heroes. Civil rights activists like Dr. Uma Chakravarti and Manoj Mitta, who had been fearless in standing up to the forces of oppression and injustice during some of the darkest days that the country had seen. The hour flew by and the actors took their bows to thundering applause and a standing ovation. We had done it! We had brought back the story of the 1984 massacre back to Delhi on the exact thirty year anniversary of the shameful event. Nothing else mattered!

The seeds of this improbable journey were planted many years ago when in the middle of studying for an exam, while at Graduate School, I started rummaging through archived copies of newspapers from a few years ago that were available at the university library. I don't remember what led me to the accounts of 1984 that I discovered. The first few headlines from US and European newspapers that I found seemed startling, because what they had to say was quite different from the narrative of 1984 that I had been exposed to while in India. The interest turned into a real thirst and I started seeking more, eager to get to the bottom of the wide divergence that I had stumbled upon from the carefully constructed narrative that I had completely bought into, just as the general public in India had, in the aftermath of 1984.

The official narrative is worth revisiting because it played a significant role in laying the groundwork for 1984 and was in large part responsible for the apathy of the general public in India that is apparent to this day. Sikhs were presented as a fractious, troublesome lot, who despite the privileged position they enjoyed in Indian society, as evidenced by their relative affluence and their visible presence in senior positions in the armed forces, the judiciary and in the civil services, were hell bent on 'tearing the fabric of the nation' apart because of their troublesome propensity to 'mix religion and politics'. It further contended that a section of Sikhs had turned to violence to further their fundamentalist religious agenda with a willingness to target innocent Hindus as part of a deliberate attempt to create terror in the minds of common people. This narrative was pervasive and enthusiastically served up by a combination of government controlled media outlets as well as a tightly controlled and subservient press. So much so that when the terrible events of June 1984 unfolded, when the Harmandir Sahib, Sikhism's preeminent place of worship was attacked by the Indian army, resulting in large scale civilian deaths, the majority of even well-meaning and sensible people including many Sikhs, breathed a sigh of relief that the 'terrorist threat' which threatened the 'unity and integrity of the nation' had finally been stemmed.

So insidious was this cleverly crafted narrative that a scant five months later, when Indira Gandhi was assassinated, an entire nation stood by and watched as its capital turned into a killing field of the kind never seen before in modern India. The same well-meaning people shuddered and averted their eyes as the carnage continued unabated in Delhi and elsewhere for several days, horrified for sure at what was happening, but at the same time surrendering to the feeling that Sikhs had in a certain sense, 'asked for it'.

I know this for a fact because as a young Sikh man, who had lived out-side the Punjab his entire life and had been completely immersed in the ubiquitous official narrative, deep in my heart, I shared that sentiment. While I felt a modicum of outrage at what had happened, the outrage was more than balanced by an abiding sense of guilt that years of listening to the official narrative had relentlessly hammered into me. Furthermore, the propaganda machine continued to propagate its carefully crafted ver-sion of events that baldly denied that the massacres in Delhi and elsewhere were organized, characterizing them as 'riots' which erupted spontane-ously after Indira Gandhi's assassination, often in reaction to Sikhs who allegedly indulged in brazen public expressions of joy at her death, even as the nation mourned!

As I started delving further into the events of 1984, accessing materi-als that had not available to me while I was in India, I remember my initial reaction as a I read a slim booklet with a stark, black cover. Complete, utter disbelief! This had to be propaganda! Developed by the most par-tisan of Sikhs, hell-bent upon discrediting the Indian government! How could this be true! After all India was a 'democracy' that took pride in its 'free press'. Who were these people who were hurling these very disturb-ing accusations at the mighty who now stalked the corridors of power in Delhi. Justice Tarkunde. Rajni Kothari. The Nagrik Ekta Manch. Names that I had not heard before.

The booklet was titled 'Who Are The Guilty' and it had been pro-duced by two Delhi based human rights organizations, The People's Union for Civil Liberties (PUCL) and the People's Union for Democratic Rights (PUDR). It was commonly referred to as 'The Black Book'. In great detail, it documented what had happened in the neighborhoods of Delhi, based on eyewitness accounts. It fearlessly named names. High ranking Congress politicians and ministers; local Congress functionar-ies; local troublemakers and toughs, who seized upon an unprecedented opportunity to rape and pillage, and ordinary citizens who inexplicably turned against Sikh neighbors, by whose side they had lived amicably for years.

I was still reeling from what I had learned upon reading the booklet, when I chanced upon a copy of an article published in *Manushi*, which was termed a 'women's magazine' and had a small readership, but in reality was a rare independent and progressive voice in the India of the mid-eighties. The article, titled 'Ganster Rule' was a fearless piece of reporting by Ms. Madhu Kishwar, the editor of the magazine, which detailed the massacre every bit as starkly and honestly as the PUCL report.

The third piece that had a profound impact on me was a paper by Dr. Veena Das, an anthropologist, published in the journal *Dædalus*. The paper titled 'Voices of Children' included interviews and field research on the children of Tilakvihar, a neighborhood in Delhi where roughly 800 Sikh families from some of the poorest and hardest hit neighborhoods of Delhi, had been settled. Dr. Das told the stories of several children who had been targets of violence during the massacre.

One of the most poignant stories in her paper was about a deaf mute boy called Avatar Singh, whose father had been hanged by a lynch mob during the pogrom. Unable to articulate his pain in any other way, the child could only mime his father's gruesome end.

In Dr. Das's own words:

One of the children in our group was Avatar, an eleven year old who had a severely damaged ear drum and was described as a deaf mute. One day as I was taking the children in a van to the site of the summer camp from their homes, Avatar became very excited. His shoulders were heaving and he was giving the impression of jumping up and down, although he was not moving at all. He forced my attention toward a tree by holding my chin and turning it in that direction. I asked what that tree was. Avatar mimed the following scene. His hands gripped an imaginary object and started to drag it. His face showed the resistance and the struggle of a person who was being dragged against his will to a terrible fate. He then stretched his hands, as if over an imaginary rope, and made a lasso of it. The lasso was sprung to catch the branch of the tree, and on the other side of the hanging rope, an imaginary noose was made. His face became that of a person around whose neck the noose had been slipped and was tightening. Then his head slumped forward and his face was that of a dead man. One of the children said that the tree was the one from which Avatar's father had been hung. It seemed to me that his body was a theater, his hands and face engaged in a conversation of gestures. Thus was memory embodied.

It often seemed to me that there was a division of labor in remembrance, as if the children who had been numbed and could not speak depended on the others to give them a voice. Balloo, perhaps five years old, never spoke. But whenever our van passed a particular spot in the locality the children would say, "That is where Balloo's father was burned alive." The crowd, it seems, had left the father after a while and though no adult had dared go to him, Balloo had run there and had held her father's hand throughout the last moments of his agony. Balloo would vehemently nod her head in affirmation, but she could never be persuaded to speak of it herself.

Twenty five years have passed since I first read these words, but to this day I vividly remember feeling shattered. We often hear about horrible things and quickly move on, because often the enormity of a tragedy gets lost in numbers and statistics. Here in sharp contrast were these stark stories of innocent children, who had suffered as no child should ever have to suffer. And in the background was a tale of the breathtaking abuse of power and that too by those who had been elected by the people to govern them, to protect them to lead them!

The writings of The PUCL/PUDR, Madhu Kishwar and Dr. Das had a profound impact on me. First of all they helped me shed my share of the collective guilt that many young Sikhs of my generation carried around after the events of 1984. They created in my heart empathy for the victims, the children in particular. My mind was in a state of ferment. I was angry and shaken and didn't quite know how to deal with what I had read and learned.

A few years before the events of 1984, I had read Gabriel Garcia Marquez's magnificent novel, One Hundred Years of Solitude, a book which thirty years later, I still count among my favorite works of fiction. In particular I remember him writing about a massacre of banana plantation workers in an unnamed Central American country, perpetrated about the company that employs them. Every bit as disturbing as the description of the massacre itself was the banana company's success at effacing all traces of the event from collective memory.

As my blood boiled, this episode from the novel played in my mind over and over again. As I seethed at the injustice of the massacre and the diabolical official attempts to bury it by palming it off as a 'riot', I started thinking of ways to respond. What poured out of me in this state of turmoil was a poem, which I decided to call Kultar's Mime, which told the stories of Avatar and Baloo and countless other children in verse.

'Kultar's Mime' was a cry of impotent rage. A lament. A plea for justice. An anguished rant that urgently wanted to be heard, lest the stories of these innocent children be forgotten, untold. Of course I had no clue if anyone would ever read the poem. But it was my way of dealing with the trauma. My way of paying homage to thousands of innocent people who were butchered merely because of who they were.

TELLING THE TALE 30 YEARS LATER :
THE EXTRAORDINARY JOURNEY OF KULTAR'S
MIME PART 2

The years passed. Like all new immigrants, I started to focus on establishing my career, which happened to be in technology, and raising a family. Kultar's Mime sat, unpublished and unread, except by a few of my closest friends and family. By 1999, I had moved to the Boston area with my family, where I got very involved with the local community with a particular focus on teaching and mentoring young people. I also started cultivating relationships with the Boston Area interfaith community. Often times, I would be asked to speak at events commemorating the 1984 massacre at Boston University and other local colleges. I would find myself dusting off the poem and reading a few stanzas as I talked about the terrible events in Delhi, which were, to my disappointment, beginning to fade from collective memory.

My young protégés would often accompany me to these events and listen to me reciting the poem. Among them was my daughter, J. Mehr Kaur.

In early 2013, Mehr who was a freshman in college then, with a focus on Theatre, came up with the idea of adapting Kultar's Mime for the stage. My initial reaction was lukewarm as I didn't really believe that a poem like Kultar's Mime could be presented effectively as a theatrical production. I was of course, delighted to be proven wrong!

Mehr came up with the idea of setting the play in an art gallery, where a group of young Western artists stumble upon the story of 1984 and decide to honor the victims by organizing an exhibition of paintings inspired the tragedy. During the exhibition, they plan to use excerpts from the poem to tell the stories of Sikh children who suffered unspeakable horrors during the massacre. Mehr shared the poem with one of her friends, Evanleigh Davis, a fellow student at Smith College and an artist, and commissioned eight original paintings based on the most powerful visual images that she perceived in the poem.

By the summer of 2013 Mehr had a script ready and had launched a theater company called Two Paths Productions, which would present Kultar's Mime as its first offering.

I remember taking my place in the audience with profoundly mixed feelings, almost twenty five years after Kultar's Mime had been written. I watched the audience enter the auditorium, taking their seats after viewing the paintings in the 'art gallery' on the stage, with the PUCL Black Book as the backdrop. Would they get it? Would they care? Would they understand what had happened and how horrible it had been for the forgotten children of the pogrom?

I need not have worried. Gasps. Tears. Stunned silence. As the young actors made Avatar and Baloo their own; as each young actor's face and body turned into a stage on which, the drama of death played, relentlessly demanding to be seen and heard.

An important milestone had been reached in the journey to tell Avatar's heart wrenching story. Of course at that time, I had no inkling that this was just the beginning.

In the months that passed, I found myself returning to the tale over and over again, my mind stirred perhaps by the powerful rendition by the young actors. I started seeking other stories of despair, in which a mere accident of birth and the ever awake monster of bigotry and hatred would conspire to heap misery upon innocents. In a sad testament to the cruel world that we live in, I found plenty, spanning culture, geography, race and time. And yet I did not stop searching until I found the tale of Kishinev, a town in modern day Moldova, in which more than a hundred years ago, the same horror had been visited upon yet another group of innocents.

The year was 1903. On April 6, the capital of the Russian province of Bessarabia erupted in violence. A horrific pogrom was organized, targeting the Jewish population of Kishinev. After three days of violence, 49 Jews were dead, 500 were wounded, 1300 homes and businesses were destroyed and 2000 families were left homeless.

The young Hebrew poet, Haim Nahman Bialik went to Kishinev to talk to survivors and report on the pogrom. Bialik wrote one of his most famous poems, 'In The City Of Slaughter' in response to the Kishinev pogrom, using searing, powerful imagery to describe the horror that descended upon the Jewish residents of the city.

I can barely describe my emotions as I read Bialik's powerful words. Of all the things that I had read, nothing came closer to arousing the same feelings I had experienced upon first reading 'The Black Book', 'Gangster Rule' and 'Voices of Children', for there were uncanny similarities between the Kishinev and Delhi pogroms. Both targeted minority communities with violence following libel, innuendo and propaganda, designed to stoke fear and hatred.

There were similarities between the poems too! The horrors described were inevitably and heart wrenchingly similar. Both narratives were also very visual in nature, conjuring up vivid, disturbing images. Even the conception and structure were similar, with the poet in both instances almost acting as a 'tour guide' and showing the reader the enormity of the horror.

Mehr too, embraced the poem and we decided to extend the play, incorporating some of Bialik's words into the Prologue as well as the last scene, uniting the stories of the two massacres and turning the play into a strong condemnation of every instance of violence against the innocent.

There is a fair amount of serendipity in how the next phase of the journey began. Early in 2014, I felt that the poem and the play ought to be published and started looking for the right person to write the foreword. In a chance conversation with Harinder Singh, an old friend and founder and former CEO of The Sikh Research Institute, a non-profit, I learned about an upcoming conference in Ottawa at Carleton University, that was to focus on the events of 1984. In subsequent conversations with Tarnjit Kaur, then also with the Sikh Research Institute, who was one of the key organizers of the conference, the notion of reviving the production and presenting it at the Ottawa conference was born. Harinder Singh decided to embrace the project and offered to present Kultar's Mime as a Sikh Research Institute production, which was a plucky decision for a small non-profit, as all that existed at the time was a script and little else! The Sikh Research Institute assigned a small development budget, and the show was cast in Boston with the modest goal of five performances, one each in Boston, New York, New Jersey, Ottawa and Toronto.

We had a small problem on our hands. Mehr, who had directed the original production and was the natural choice to direct the expanded version of the play, was completely tied up in the summer at an internship at the Glimmerglass Opera Festival in New York. In the fall, she had registered for a very intensive semester at the National Theater Institute, which made her completely unavailable. We contemplated hiring an outside director, until Mehr suggested that I should step in, given my familiarity with the material. I had dabbled in theater of course; in fact I had directed Mehr in her first play ever when she was all of ten, a historical play in Punjabi that I had written. When I demurred, concerned about the difference in directing a bunch of middle-schoolers versus a cast of professional actors, she somewhat cheekily handed me a slim volume titled *Notes On Directing*, by Frank Hauser and Russel Reich and assured me that 'things would be fine'!

We started rehearsing in late July. The response to our audition notice had been encouraging and several fine actors showed up. The five who were eventually selected, had a few things in common. In addition to being solid actors, Addison Williams, Allison Matteodo, Cat Roberts, Christine Scherer and Michelle Finston had all been asked why they were interested in Kultar's Mime, which was as off the beaten path as a project possibly could be, relative to the mainstream productions that they had been involved with thus far. Each one of them in response expressed the sentiment that this was a story they felt was clearly worth telling, notwithstanding the cultural distance that separated them from it. This was truly the foundation on which the eventual success of the production was built.

For the next several weeks, this group of young actors, our newly hired Stage Manager, Ross Magnant and Poornima Kirby, Assistant Director and Movement Designer, all of whom had never so much as encountered a Sikh before in a social setting, immersed themselves in dramaturgical work, receiving detailed presentations and lectures on Sikh history in addition to all the works that had inspired the original poem that the play was based on. They developed a nuanced understanding of the Sikh worldview and its alignment with the underdog in every situation and participated in a finely grained analysis of the political fortunes of the Sikhs in the last century, which laid the groundwork of the terrible excesses of 1984. They also watched films like Kaya Taran, which sensitively portrayed the pain of a community and the triumph of compassion over evil.

In August, 2014, I took a short break from rehearsals and made a quick trip to India, primarily to bring my elderly parents back with me to the US, as their immigration formalities had been completed. Even though our initial budget was really insufficient, even for the five performances that we had planned, deep in my heart, I had been dreaming rather audaciously about taking the production to Delhi on the 30 year anniversary of the massacre. It did seem like a daunting task. After all I knew nothing about the theater scene in Delhi and furthermore, it was entirely possible that the city that had chosen to bury the memory of this unsavory chapter in its history would have no interest whatsoever in seeing it back in the spotlight!

I was in Delhi for exactly one day and I ended up meeting two extraordinary people, to whom Kultar's Mime will always be indebted.

My first meeting was with Professor Kuljeet Singh, who teaches English at Delhi University. Kuljeet Singh also runs Atelier Expressions, a well-established Delhi based Theater Company that is known for its innovative productions. Within all of fifteen minutes Kuljeet had embraced the project with such alacrity and enthusiasm that now, coming to Delhi with the play was just a matter of fundraising and logistics! I left the meeting greatly energized and a little nervous because what had until now been a pipe dream was actually starting to take shape!

The second meeting that day was no less significant. Later that evening, I sat across an energetic, bird-like woman, probably in her seventies, in her living room, answering rapid fire questions about the nature of Kultar's Mime and my motivation in trying to revive a conversation that was all but dead. After her curiosity was satisfied, she shared her journey with me. Her name was Uma Chakravarti; she was a retired academic, celebrated as one of India's best known feminists and a tireless crusader for human rights for decades. A longtime resident of Delhi, Dr. Chakravarti, then a Professor at Miranda House, had experienced the terrible events of 1984 personally. She had been at the forefront of relief work and had extensively toured the shattered neighborhoods in Delhi where Sikhs had been attacked, painstakingly documenting their stories. These stories were published in a book titled, *The Delhi Riots: Three Days in the Life of a Nation*, co—authored with one of her former students Nandita Haksar, who went on to become one of India's best known civil rights attorneys. She also mentored Shonali Bose, another student who put up a street play about the events in the aftermath and went on to make the acclaimed film Amu, probably the best known cinematic work on 1984.

I would be remiss in not sharing a small anecdote about a prior conversation that we had on the phone, before I travelled to Delhi. I had already approached other Indian academics as well, many of them of leftist bent, who had done excellent work on 1984, to talk about Kultar's Mime. I have to confess that I often encountered a modicum of suspicion about my motivation. Perhaps they felt that Kultar's Mime was an attempt to stir up trouble, thirty years after the fact, and their wariness had mildly dampened my enthusiasm. When I called Dr. Chakravarti and introduced myself and the project, I hastened to add that my concern was primarily focused human rights and that Kultar's Mime was not intended to be political. At which point I remember receiving a sharp rebuke on the phone. 'Of course it's political!' she snapped, 'And I completely approve!'

There was no better sounding board than Dr. Chakravarti and when she enthusiastically endorsed the project and offered to invite many of the leading civil rights activists of Delhi, who had been working with the survivors of 1984 for almost three decades, the decision was made.

Somehow, my team of young actors from halfway across the world was going to get to Delhi to tell this story. It certainly felt that the Universe wanted this to happen!

TELLING THE TALE 30 YEARS LATER:
THE EXTRAORDINARY JOURNEY OF KULTAR'S
MIME PART 3

Back in Boston, our rehearsals continued and the production began to take shape. As a corporate refugee from the tech world thrust into the arts, I did what I had been trained to do. I relied heavily on Mehr's original staging and advice, choosing to not reinvent the wheel, and turned to people with complementary skills for help. Poornima, who had a strong background in movement based theater, was a huge help as she worked with the actors to develop a toolbox and vocabulary that became integral to the production. Her contributions far exceeded just the movement design and she was also able to very effectively incorporate the puppetry skills of Michelle, one of the actors, into the staging. Ross, our Stage Manager, who is one of the most affable people I have ever had the pleasure of working with, and a fine actor himself, also contributed in many significant ways. The entire cast was energetic, hardworking and clearly very motivated and in late September, somewhat miraculously from my perspective, it seemed that we were ready!

We opened on September 27, 2014 at the Cabot House Theater at Harvard University. The small, intimate theater was full. The audience was an interesting mix of Harvard students and academics as well as members of the community. I was of course standing in the back, my heart in my mouth, with absolutely no inkling of how the audience was going to react. The response was overwhelming! The audience was engaged and very emotional, which was a fine testament to the hard work of my brilliant cast and crew. Very spontaneously, two Harvard undergraduates, Herman Kaur and Gurbani Kaur, stepped up to organize an informal 'talk-back' with me and the cast. This was the genesis of a component of the Kultar's Mime experience that over time, became every bit as compelling as the play itself.

The audience included Dr. Diana Eck, Harvard Professor and founder of the Harvard Pluralism project. Dr. Eck and I have had the opportunity to interact many times over the last decade in various inter-faith settings and she is a person that I deeply admire. Her nuanced and sensitive response to the play greatly enriched the talk-back and really helped me comprehend the true potential of the production. The admixture of compassion, energy and yes, anger that poured out of the audience during the talk-back made it abundantly clear that Kultar's Mime had the potential to become a powerful tool in response to violence and oppression.

Our 'big' Boston performance was scheduled for the next day at the Armory in Somerville, a much larger performance space. We had more than 300 people signed up for the show. A week earlier I had spoken at one of the Boston Area Gurdwaras (A Sikh place of worship) about the upcoming play and I was standing in the lobby with some young volunteers, registering people for the event. As a Sikh, whenever I am involved with any kind of gathering, I feel an irresistible urge to arrange for food. My sentiments are in no way unique; the pull of Guru Ka Langar (the Sikh community kitchen), I know for a fact is pervasive within the community. I had broached the notion to a couple of local Gurdwaras, but unfortunately nothing seemed to be falling in place despite good intentions all around. As I stood in the lobby of the Everett Gurdwara, a young man walked up and started studying our poster intently and then turned to me and asked if he could support the project in any way. It turned out that he ran a couple of restaurants in the Boston area and after a brief conversation he enthusiastically signed up to provide food for all the attendees for our upcoming performance. I was delighted but not overly surprised because the magic of the Guru Ka Langar makes its appearance often in unexpected ways!

The Somerville performance was no less successful than our debut. We had a full house which included elected officials, academics, interfaith leaders, journalist and many community members. The audience engagement was powerful and the very cathartic talk back was moderated by Dr.

Amit Basole of The University of Massachusetts, Boston. Beena Sarwar, a well-known Pakistani journalist, who was in the audience, went on to write a powerful review of the production. Pushpir Singh's delicious food, offered with love and generosity, made the evening even more memorable for all of our guests.

As we were readying to tour with the show, our fundraising activities had started in earnest. We launched a crowdfunding campaign on Indiegogo and I quietly started soliciting friends and family for contributions to fund our trip to India, which by now, we were fully committed to. The success of the funding campaign was unexpected and literally in a few weeks, we had enough money to take the production to India. The reputation that the Sikh Research Institute enjoys for doing stellar, meaningful work was a huge factor in the enthusiastic support we received from the community.

Our India tour was starting to take shape. Kuljeet was quite insistent that we perform in Delhi on the exact thirty year anniversary of the massacre and he had arranged three performances in Delhi on October 30 and 31 and November 1. While we were doing our dramaturgical work, the cast and crew that learned about the important place that the Sri Harmandir Sahib in Amritsar, (popularly known as The Golden Temple) occupies in the Sikh psyche. I had promised them that if we ever got to India, we would definitely travel to Amritsar to visit the Sri Harmandir Sahib. I figured that if we were traveling to Amritsar, it might be a good idea to perform there as well. I got in touch with S. Hirday Paul Singh, son of the late S. Gurbaksh Singh, the well-known Punjabi writer, who also happens to be my uncle, to seek his help and he was able to arrange a performance for us at the Punjab Natshala, Amritsar's premier theater venue.

S. Hirday Paul Singh also introduced the project to Kewal Dahaliwal, who is presently one of the best known theater personalities in the Punjab, recently having received the National Sangeet Naatak Akademi award in 2013. Mr. Dahaliwal very generously decided to invite us to Chandigarh to perform at the Punjab Arts Council, the premier arts organization in the Punjab.

The pipe dream was now very real and we already had five performances booked in India! However, before we go to India, we had five North American touring performances to look forward to.

We got a rousing welcome from the community in New Jersey. Close to three hundred people, many with young children in tow came to the performance at Rutgers University. Our talk-back was moderated by Shruti Devgan, a doctoral student at Rutgers who has done extensive research on the 1984 massacre. The Rutgers show was particularly poignant for the cast because for the first time they encountered survivors of the 1984 carnage, who shared powerful personal stories that perhaps fully drove home the import of the project that they had stumbled into. The New York City performance was at an old Off Broadway venue called the Actors Temple Theater, which is right in the theater district and has a lot of character. It also happens to be housed in a synagogue, which, given the connection of the play to the Kishinev pogrom, made this a very special venue for me. The performance was moderated by Sapreet Kaur, Executive Director of the Sikh Coalition, which was also sponsoring the event. The cast once again encountered many first-hand accounts from survivors and Sikhs whose families had been shattered by the violence. The audience had a large contingent of young people and it became apparent from the thoughtful and nuanced comments in the talkback, that the production was starting to become very effective at engaging a new generation of Sikhs and non-Sikhs who had been born after the events of 1984.

Our next destination was Canada with our first show at the conference at Carleton University in Ottawa that had provided the initial impetus for the production to be revived. The Ottawa talk-back, which was moderated by Dr. Richard Mann, the organizer of the conference, was memorable for many reasons. Jaspreet Singh, the author of the acclaimed novel, Helium, perhaps the first work of fiction in English about 1984 was in the audience. A Sikh gentleman, probably in his early fifties got up to speak very eloquently about his personal experiences in 1984; his family had suffered tremendously and it was apparent that the trauma was still fresh and ever present in his mind. His son, in his early 20s, was also in the audience. Later, we learned that father and son, until that day, had never had a conversation about 1984! The Canada trip was memorable in other ways as well. For the first time, the cast was introduced to the delight that is Sikh hospitality as they were feted and fed by the community. The Brampton performance drew a mostly Sikh audience and emotions ran high as the audience relived the horrors of 1984.

The third performance, in Toronto at the Miles Nadal Jewish Community Center (JCC), I will remember fondly as one of my favorites for several reasons. Navneet Kaur, a young Sikh woman from Toronto, with an abiding interest in theater had earlier introduced Kultar's Mime to the JCC, emphasizing the universal theme of the play. The JCC found the concept interesting enough to become a partner for the Toronto performance. The Toronto Kultar's Mime had been promoted by the JCC within its membership and as a result we ended up with an extremely diverse audience. There was also a huge contingent of Sikh University students, who like the NYC audience engaged with the play in a very thoughtful manner.

In the audience was my good friend and mentor T. Sher Singh, who had earlier distinguished himself in a long legal career as the first Keshadhari (a Sikh with unshorn hair and a turban) lawyer in Canada. In his current avatar, T. Sher Singh is a writer and edits the widely read online culture magazine, SikhChic. Roughly a year ago, I had started writing a weekly column for SikhChic, which had provided me with a terrific platform to address just about anything from my personal, very Sikh perspective. I had written on current events; I had published poetry and fiction on SikhChic and had written two series of articles, one called the Darbar

Chronicles about the men and women who surrounded Maharaja Ranjit Singh during his reign and the second, The Diaspora Diaries, stories of Sikh men and women who embodied the one hundred and twenty year history of the Sikhs in America.

I have already acknowledged Harinder Singh of SikhRi, Professor Kuljeet Singh and Dr. Uma Chakravarti as some of the individuals who made Kultar's Mime journey possible. T. Sher Singh definitely belongs in that group as well!

I can never forget the encouragement, sage advice and help that I have received from this extraordinary man over the past couple of years. His appreciation for my work has really fueled me to embrace ambitious projects that in hindsight seemed quixotic! His response was no different when I broached the notion of publishing Kultar's Mime and reviving the stage production. The thing that I appreciate most about him is his ability to dream large and to inject that broad vision into every conversation that we have had about new projects. He has introduced me to many interesting people and has enhanced my network tremendously and has been tireless and generous in using his own network to enhance the reach of Kultar's Mime. We actually had our first face to face meeting at the Toronto performance of the play. I was eagerly awaiting his feedback as T Sher Singh, who is no milquetoast, is passionate and knowledgeable about theater and I was confident that I would get an honest opinion from him about the production. The man responded by calling the performance Shakespearean, which to me, an avowed Shakespeare nerd, was the pinnacle of praise, and put a Cheshire cat smile on my face for the rest of the evening!

The cast, after the performance was mobbed by the University students; watching that rich interaction unfold was unequivocally one of the highlights of the tour.

TELLING THE TALE 30 YEARS LATER :
THE EXTRAORDINARY JOURNEY OF KULTAR'S
MIME PART 4

India beckoned!

The Delhi performances were emotional and spectacular. Twenty-five years ago, when I wrote the lines 'When I walk the streets of Delhi today I still see blood mixed with the dust', I was being only marginally hyperbolical. Ever since I became aware of what had really transpired in Delhi in 1984, my relationship with the city has always been troubled. I just cannot feel at ease in Delhi. As I look at unfamiliar faces of strangers scurrying past me in the streets, I cannot help thinking. Maybe that is one of the men who looted or raped or killed during those terrible days! The pall of 1984 is ever present, no matter who I am with or what I am doing. I must say however, that the pall did lift somewhat by the mere act of bringing the play to the city where these ghastly things had happened.

We were in Delhi only for a few days, but as my cast and crew had never been in India before, I was eager to show them as much of Delhi as I possibly could. Our sightseeing started on a rather strange note when the cast was mobbed by the throngs at India Gate, mostly young men, who rather aggressively insisted on being photographed with them. It took my most curmudgeonly scowls and in some cases sharp rebukes to keep them at bay! We visited Humayun's Tomb, a beautiful and serene monument and there the cast had the honor of meeting Dr. Uma Chakravarti who instantly became a mentor to everyone, holding forth effortlessly on a variety of topics and clucking with annoyance upon hearing of the celebrity status that the cast had acquired with the gawkers at India Gate!

During our dramaturgical work, I had told the cast about S. Harvinder Singh Phoolka, the indefatigable lawyer who had been seeking justice for the victims of 1984 for thirty long years. Mr. Phoolka was extremely busy because of all the events in progress relating to the thirty year anniversary of the massacre, but was kind enough to make some time for us. It was a proud moment for the cast and me, when we briefly visited with him at the Delhi High Court.

The Delhi shows behind us, we piled into a small bus we had rented and made our way to Chandigarh. Traveling by road in northern India is always an interesting experience even for seasoned India hands. The most memorable aspect, I am sure, for the cast was this uniquely Indian game of chicken that vehicles play on undivided highways with traffic bearing down upon them from the opposite direction as they desperately try to overtake cars and trucks ahead of them. The delights of roadside dhaba (little eateries lining highways) food that we sampled, I am sure, were no less memorable.

The Chandigarh performance was significant for several reasons. Until then, we had organized each performance on our own, booking the venues ourselves and making all the arrangements. In Chandigarh, we were the guests of the Punjab Arts Council, the apex body that oversees all the government run arts organizations in the Punjab. They had offered the space to us free of charge and had promoted the play widely in the city. We had Kewal Dhaliwal and Bibi Harjinder Kaur, who runs the Punjab Arts Council to thank for the generous invitation. The audience that turned up did not disappoint us. Artists, journalists, academics, activists, government officials, officers in the Police and Army, both serving and retired, made up the bulk of the audience. The reaction was emotional and the outpouring of love and gratitude, directed towards my youthful cast, who was telling a story that was profoundly meaningful to this mostly Sikh audience, was truly humbling.

So overwhelming was the reaction of the audience that it prompted a prominent media figure, who shall remain nameless, and who to be fair, had suffered personally because of the violence leading up to 1984, allegedly at the hands of Sikh militants, to launch into a diatribe, in which she somewhat incoherently fulminated against the 'American' actors from 'the land of Coca Cola' telling the story and berated the audience for 'fawning' upon them. Carried away by emotion, she criticized the play for not addressing violence in the Punjab, calling it 'one sided', prompting other members of the audience to get extremely angry with her. I was of course insistent that she be allowed to have her say, but did not have the opportunity to respond to her, because she stalked out of the theater right after her outburst!

Her rantings did make me reflect on the pervasiveness of the official narrative which continues to influence intelligent and often well-meaning people to take breathtakingly bigoted and hateful positions even today.

I feel that an important digression from the story of our journey is in order.

There is no denying the fact that the political situation in the Punjab leading up to 1984 and after 1984 was extremely murky. There is no denying that Punjab was in the grip of terrible violence in those days. There were many conflicting agendas at play; center stage was the rivalry between the ruling Akalis and the Congress party; with the utter collapse of law and order, there was certainly an undercurrent of vigilantism and fundamentalism in the Punjab with the controversial Sant Jarnail Singh Bhinderanwale at its center; guns were everywhere and the media was choked with incessant stories of 'Sikh Militants' out to terrorize and kill innocent Hindus. The 'foreign hand' of Pakistan and its role in fomenting trouble in the Punjab was constantly touted as well.

Startling revelations over many years clearly show that there were many sources of violence in the Punjab. Most notorious of these were the Punjab Police as well as Indian paramilitary forces, who terrorized the populace with impunity. There were certainly Sikh militants in the mix, who were driven by ideology. In addition it is now well documented that there were death squads created by the government whose charter was to commit violent acts in the name of Sikh militancy. Making an already murky situation worse was a large criminal element that gleefully exploited to chaos to further its own ends.

Unraveling the mess that was the Punjab in the mid-eighties is a subject worthy of much deeper study but it is clearly beyond the scope of this essay! I would point interested readers to the work of Joyce Pettigrew (*The Sikhs of the Punjab: Unheard Voices of State and Guerilla Violence*), Cynthia Keppley Mahmood (*Fighting for Faith and Nation: Dialogues with Sikh Militants*) and Ram Narayan Kumar (*Reduced to Ashes - The Insurgency and Human Rights in Punjab*) as a starting point.

One assertion however, I can make very confidently in response to the woman who got up to spew hatred in Chandigarh! There is no 'other side' to a massacre of innocents. It does not matter who we are talking about. The Jews of Kishinev, The Sikhs of Delhi, The Muslims of Godhra, The Yazidis of Iraq and countless others who have been targeted simply because of who they were. It truly does not matter what the situation in the Punjab was before 1984. Nothing can justify the massacre that the play depicts. Bringing up 'the other side' is merely hateful code for justifying the massacre of innocents. I absolutely do not believe that the woman who ranted about the 'the other side' would explicitly or overtly condone the Delhi massacre; in fact I happen to know that she is an intelligent, well read and compassionate person whose heart is in the right place. This really speaks to the insidious nature of the narrative of hatred, xenophobia, canard and innuendo, which can take decent human beings and turn them into apologists for genocide!

On a lighter note, there is one more Chandigarh story that is worth telling. Seated in the front row was Pandit Yashpal Ji, the senior most exponent of the Agra Khayal Gharana (a school of North Indian Vocal Classical music). A redoubtable musician of note with a personality to match, Pandit Ji had been Mehr's vocal Ustad (teacher) since she had outgrown my ability to groom her further, musically speaking. Now Pandit Ji and Mehr had never actually met as his lessons had been delivered exclusively over Skype. Despite being an extremely tough teacher with at times a somewhat curmudgeonly outlook, Pandit Ji had grown very fond of Mehr over the two years that he taught her. Of course Pandit Ji was very disappointed that his protégé was not traveling with the production, but he was very excited to attend the play she had created. At one point during the talkback, Pandit Ji seemed to get somewhat agitated and I could tall that he was trying to say something, albeit not very loudly. Later I learned that he was expressing his indignation at the perceived shortchanging of his protégé. He felt that my acknowledgement of Mehr as the co-director had been a bit anemic and he was determined to correct it!

From Chandigarh, we proceeded to a tiny village outside Amritsar, which has a rich and interesting history well worth recounting.

The village, called Preet Nagar of the Hamlet of Love was established decades ago by a visionary born in the Punjab in 1895, who was greatly inspired by the writings of Thoreau, Emerson and Whitman. Sardar Gurbaksh Singh started his career as an engineer, studying at the Thompson College in Roorkee before traveling to the US to further his education by studying Civil Engineering at The University of Michigan, Ann Arbor.

During a few years spent working at Youngstown Ohio after graduating, the young Gurbaksh Singh found a mentor in an older woman named Mrs. MacAtree who was instrumental in developing his love for literature by introducing him to masters like Victor Hugo, Ibsen, Leo Tolstoy, H.G. Wells, Thomas Hardy, Joseph Conrad, Anatole France, Walt Whitman, Emerson, Nietzsche, Goethe, Kant, Miller and numerous other writers. The young man gradually turned from a bibliophile to writer and started writing short stories and plays in English!

Towards the end of 1923 he somewhat reluctantly abandoned the new friendships that had so nurtured and inspired him and returned to India. By 1934, fully committed to a life of letters, he had started the groundbreaking Punjabi journal, Preet Lari, which loosely translates to 'chainlinks of love'. While living in Lahore, his ideas started attracting other writers and artists who bought into his Walden-like vision of *a life of simplicity, independence, magnanimity, and trust* and the idea of Preet Nagar, the 'hamlet of love', was born.

It was perhaps fitting that the land to create this utopian settlement of artists and thinkers, was acquired with the help of Dhani Ram Chatrik, who is considered to be one of the fathers of modern Punjabi poetry. Roughly halfway between Lahore, the most important city in the Punjab, and nearby Amritsar, the citadel of the Sikh faith, lay a tract of land that used to house a Mughal guest house, which served as a resting place for the Empress Noor Jahan on her journeys to Kashmir. After the death of the Emperor Jahangir, the land had passed to the family of an old retainer that Chatrik was a part of. A hundred and seventy-five acres were purchased through Chartik's good offices and Preet Nagar came into existence in 1938.

The Mughal guest-house by then was in ruins. All that remained was a pond spread over two acres and a brick wall four foot wide and eight foot high, encircling an area of seventeen acres, in which stood an imposing two story mansion built with thin but strong baked bricks. There was also a well with a Persian wheel. The wall was demolished and with is ancient bricks, eight new houses were built. The mansion was turned into a recreational facility, and the pond was filled up and converted into a play-house for children. Public bathrooms were built around the Persian wheel. Two families were asked to share each house and on June 7, 1938, the first settlers moved in. The first inhabitants included Gurbaksh Singh, the noted Punjabi novelist Nanak Singh, the poet Piara Singh Sehrai, the short story writer Naurang Singh, the humorist Piara Singh Data and others such as Giani Harbhajan Singh, Deen Dayal, Kartar Singh Sachdev, D.C.Dawar, Chaman Lal, Amar Singh, Bakhshish Singh, Gurbachan Singh Khurana, Dalip Singh, Tara Singh Malhotra and Harcharan Singh.

The partition of India in 1947 brought an abrupt end to the beautiful utopian experiment that had been Preet Nagar, largely because of safety concerns stemming from its proximity to the new border with a hostile neighbor, Pakistan. Sardar Gurbaksh Singh, however continued to live there and publish Preet Lari, which continued to be the premier literary magazine in Punjabi.

Our tour bus slipped into the tiny village and my crew spilled out. We were at the Gurbaksh Singh Nanak Singh Foundation, a non-profit dedicated to the memory of Sardar Gurbaksh Singh and S. Nanak Singh. Earlier, as had I corresponded with S. Hirday Paul Singh to set up our Amritsar performance, he had shared with me, an intriguing suggestion made by Kewal Dhaliwal that we perform in Preet Nagar in addition to performing at Amritsar. I received the suggestion with mixed feelings as I knew that the likely audience in the village was going to be almost exclusively non English speaking and I was concerned that a play in English, in verse to boot, may not be able to engage its interest. When I expressed my concerns, S. Hirday Paul Singh responded with Kewal Dhaliwal's tongue in cheek response that if not anything else, the villagers would show up to 'behold the faces of the white actors'!

6 p.m. approached rapidly and the audience started filtering in. Timidly. Farmers and their wives and their daughters and their sons. Day laborers, still dusty from their long day at work. Many young men, who had traveled from neighboring villages, miles away, mostly drawn by curiosity. Unseen by anyone, others slipped in too. The spirits of the greatest artists that the Punjab has known in modern times. Novelists, essayists, painters, actors, poets and their muses. Artists whose work was celebrated in their lifetimes not just in the Punjab but all over India and indeed all over the world. The founders of the Hamlet of Love!

And what a performance it was! Pin drop silence. Thundering applause at the end! As in Chandigarh, a spontaneous outpouring of love for the cast. Belying my fears, the audience sat transfixed throughout the play and engaged with it no differently from our most 'sophisticated' audiences in the major cities of the US, UK, Canada or India!

After sampling the idyllic delights of life in the rural Punjab, including close encounters with buffalos and other farm animals, we left Preet Nagar the following morning and went to visit the Sri Harmandir Sahib in Amritsar.

Anyone who ever has visited the Sri Harmandir Sahib has experienced the effect of its serene beauty will know exactly how we felt when we passed through its lofty gates to enter to the most peaceful promenade in the world. We took a moment to orient ourselves and talked about where the Indian Army's mightiest tanks would have rolled in from to start their assault on the Akal Takhat (a building inside the Golden Temple complex, which has historically been the seat of Sikh temporal authority) thirty years ago; a sobering moment as we silently acknowledged the power of the extraordinary journey that had brought us here.

The parikarma (encircling promenade) of the Sri Harmandir Sahib was as beautiful as ever, as it perfectly framed the shimmering vision in the middle of the pool that it encloses. Our little band made its way towards the entrance to the Sri Harmandir Sahib. It was the top of the hour and a new Ragi Jatha (group of Sikh minstrels) was about to begin singing, as was evident from the tapping sounds of a tabla (drums) being tuned, that reverberated around us.

A masterful Alap (free unmetered exploration of a Raga, a melodic scale from a system of musical scales that forms the basis of both Indian Classical Music and Gurmat Sangeet or Sikh Sacred Music) began and I listened, rapt. I was not sure if my young companions were listening as well, their attention undoubtedly drawn to the panoply of unfamiliar sights around them. My face broke out in a joyous smile as I recognized the melody. It was Raga Tilang. I do have favorites when it comes to Ragas and I must confess that Tilang is clearly and unequivocally one of them.

The unexpected joy of listening to a shabads (hymn) in Tilang on a chance visit to the Sri Harmandir Sahib would be enough to make me smile.

But today, there was more!

Our visit to the Sri Harmandir Sahib, was not the end of the journey of Kultar's Mime. It was a halting place and an important one. For me personally, our visit that day was a promise kept. A promise made, early in our process of crafting the production that had brought us here.

Recognizing early on that I had been blessed with a team that was super smart, curious and willing to engage with the arduous task of trying to understand the ethos of a people, driven by a desire to tell their story in a credible manner, I threw everything that I possibly could at my band. Starting from the beginning of Sikh history. The principles that the Guru's lived and died by. The forging of a new identity. The tumultuous history of the eighteenth century as a fledgling faith committed to fighting for the underdog was forced to fight for its own survival as well. Its improbable ascension to power and glory and its inevitable fall and resurrection. The scars and wounds of history from the fifteenth century to modern times.

Of course the Sri Harmandir Sahib loomed large in this narrative, given its larger than life role in defining Sikh identity and its position as the stage where some of the most dramatic moments in the history of the Sikhs have played out. If we ever get to India, I had said, cautioning everyone that it was highly unlikely that we ever would, I will definitely take you to the Golden Temple.

And here we were on that day!

My joy at hearing Tilang being sung, also needs to be explained.

As I was auditioning the Kultar's Mime team, the germ of an idea was forming in my mind. Mehr Kaur had already incorporated painting into the production and poetry of course was an integral part of the play. A lovely melody had been used in the original production, but somewhere along the way, we started exploring the possibility of incorporating some elements of Gurmat Sangeet (traditional Sikh sacred music) into the new version of the play.

Maybe it was coincidence, maybe it was not, but most of the actors who had been cast were singers with lovely voices and fairly early on in the rehearsal process, they were introduced to Tilang, which to me, beautifully evoked the mood of the play. A few rehearsals later, it was clear to me that this was going to work.

There were rough spots for sure. The use of the two flavors of the Nishad (the sixth note) and the meend (glide) from the Gandhar (the third note) to the Shadja (the first or base note) were challenging at first, but the crew ploughed on gamely.

And then something wonderful happened. A natural leader emerged in the form of Christine Scherer, who has a beautiful voice and a lot of experience singing in the western context.

In addition to a brief exploration of Raga Tilang, which we used in a couple of scenes, we also incorporated one of my favorite Shabads from the writings of Sri Guru Nanak Sahib (The First Sikh Guru) : Yakk Arz Guftam Pes To Dar Gos Kun Kartar.

Having had some experience teaching westerners how to sing traditional Gurmat Sangeet compositions, I had no illusions about the difficulty of the process, when we started. The cast of Kultar's Mime definitely rose to the challenge and with Christine in the lead, they were able to render the melody quite well by the time our show opened at Harvard in late September, not singing the text but humming the tune.

Christine and I continued to work on the Shabad (hymn), spending some 1-1 time in addition to our regular rehearsals and I was delighted when she expressed a desire to get familiar with the text as well. She felt that being able to sing the words would give her a better handle on the melody and I wholeheartedly agreed.

After we arrived in India, on the day of the first show we had set aside some time for a rehearsal. During the rehearsal Christine came up to me and announced that she was ready to sing a line or two from the shabad in the India shows. I readily agreed but gulped inside! After all we were now performing in India, before Sikh audiences, which would invariably include many aficionados and practitioners of Gurmat Sangeet. How would they react? Would it be incongruous to hear an obviously western voice with an American accent singing lines form Gurbani on stage?

I need not have worried. Christine nailed it!

Numerous people came up to me after our India shows commenting on how wonderfully this young woman sang the lines from the shabad and what a beautiful voice she had! I remember an audience member in Delhi or Chandigarh saying that he had goose bumps!

All these thoughts ran through my mind as I stood with my little band on the Parikarma and listened to the beautiful melody in Raga Tilang and the impossibility of our journey struck me again.

And then I smiled. Impossible journeys too, can be completed if one just believes. And at the end, there are fabulous rewards.

The Shabad in Raga Tilang, as we visited the Sri Harmandir Sahib was such a reward. For Christine. And for Michelle, Cat, Addison, Allison & Ross!

Our performance in Amritsar that evening was every bit as magical as the Chandigarh and Preet Nagar performances. An erudite audience that included Kewal Dhaliwal, once again showered the cast with accolades and affection.

Of course no visit to Amritsar would be complete without sampling the famous culinary delights of the city! Before heading back to Delhi the same night we feasted on magnificent traditional Punjabi food at the well-known Bharawn Da Hotel!

The tour wasn't quite over yet. Two days later, we landed at Heathrow, where a large van belonging to the Leeds Gurdwara was waiting to whisk us to Huddersfield in Yorkshire. Tim Bhullar, a successful businessman from Huddersfield had stumbled upon Kultar's Mime on the Sikh Coalition website and had expressed interest in bringing Kultar's Mime to the UK. Over the next couple of days the team was once more the recipient of the full force of Punjabi hospitality! The following morning we were driven to the BBC studio in Leeds, where we had a live appearance on the Nihal Show, one of the most popular radio talk shows on the BBC, focused on the South Asian community. The same evening we had fully sold out performance at Huddersfield University followed by a performance the next day at a lovely venue in Birmingham, called The Drum. Both shows featured a large contingent of young Sikhs who just like our audiences in New York and Toronto, engaged emotionally and powerfully with the play. I believe the Sikh community in the UK, in general is much more aware of the events of 1984, perhaps because of the role local organizations have played in keeping them alive in the collective memory of the community.

TELLING THE TALE 30 YEARS LATER :
THE EXTRAORDINARY JOURNEY OF KULTAR'S
MIME PART 5

Our next stop was the SikhLens Festival at Chapman University in LA. In the words of the organizers : "Sikhlens seeks to provide an outlet for sharing Sikh heritage and culture with the rest of the world by creating awareness for work that is 'Sikh-centric', showcasing talent, and instilling pride in the community. The festival seeks work from artists in a variety of fields, including but not limited to movies, books, music, and art. It creates appropriate avenues for this work to be shared with the rest of the world ". SikhLens 2014 was focused on 1984, making Kultar's Mime a great fit for the festival. I had been in correspondence with Bicky Singh, the main organizer for several months and we had decided to perform the play twice at the festival, once during their opening Gala for a small selected audience and a second time for a larger audience of festival attendees.

SikhLens is a labor of love for Bicky Singh and he has spent years developing a deep relationship with Chapman University which seems to have paid rich dividends. The SikhLens Festival easily outshines any 'Sikh' cultural event that I have ever been to, in terms of both the level of organization and the content presented.

Our opening performance was, of all places, in a library, which had a small impromptu stage and no stage lighting. I was a bit apprehensive because of the ad-hoc nature of the space, but I need not have worried. The audience was completely enthralled and in one of the most poignant moments of the tour, several non-South-Asian professors from Chapman came up to me after the performance, and confessed that they had been so moved that they could not contain their tears. The second performance, at a much larger space at the Dodge Film School was equally emotional. Particularly gratifying was the feedback of several artists and filmmakers, whose brilliant work we had enjoyed tremendously during the festival.

One of them in particular, deserves mention. Michael Singh is a California based documentary filmmaker of Dutch, German and Sikh descent, who was brought up in India. His powerful documentary, Riding The Tiger, which is based on his personal recollections of the violence he witnessed in Delhi in 1984, was screened at the festival. His enthusiasm for Kultar's Mime and his generous praise was fully matched by mine for his documentary. Riding the Tiger is yet unfinished and I am eagerly awaiting its release, most likely on PBS in the US. Michael is also one of the several individuals who have seen the play, who have suggested that it be repurposed for film and shown possibly on PBS or The BBC. This is definitely one of the projects that Mehr and I have on our list of things to do after the Kultar's Mime tour comes to an end.

After a short break for Thanksgiving we were on a plane again for London. We had been invited to participate in two events commemorating the violence of 1984. The first one was to be at the Wolver Hampton Civic Center in the West Midlands. In addition to human rights activists from the UK and India, members of the British and EU Parliaments and local leaders, the organizers, Jas Singh and Dabinderjit Singh of the Sikh Federation, UK, were expecting a gathering larger than a thousand, which would definitely be a new experience for the Kultar's Mime team!

It was a memorable experience! Busloads of audience members, some of whom had traveled great distances to be at the event! Absolute pin drop silence as more than a thousand pairs of eyes, many wet with tears, made the pain of Kultar and his young friends their own. The entire performance was telecast live and watched by thousands more on television all over Europe.

The second performance during our short trip was no less memorable. We returned to London where we were scheduled to present Kultar's Mime at British Parliament.

One of the personal highlights of the tour for me, actually had nothing to do with the play! A few years earlier, I had undergone initiation to enter the ranks of the Khalsa, the order created by Guru Gobind Singh Sahib, the Tenth Sikh Guru in 1699. In addition to embracing a well-defined code of conduct and personal discipline all initiates also commit to wearing on their persons the five prescribed symbols of the Khalsa, one of which is a sword, known as a 'Kirpan' or 'Siri Sahib'.

In the post 9-11 world, hypersensitive to concerns about security, carrying a Siri Sahib on one's person often forces a choice upon a Khalsa. A Siri Sahib for instance, is never acceptable at a security checkpoint at an airport. In the US, as I am sure is the case in many countries, a Siri Sahib may not be worn wile entering various public buildings, courthouses etc. Needless to say, I do find the restriction irksome and I deal with if by simply staying away from places where a Siri Sahib would not be allowed. Of course I am forced to compromise when I have to board a plane for instance, but there is always an accompanying twinge of unease. A couple of years ago, I was invited to an event at The White House, celebrating the birth anniversary of Guru Nanak Sahib, the First Sikh Guru. I would have been delighted to attend, but when I was told that my Siri Sahib would definitely not make it through White House security, I politely declined.

I had been told that the UK, given its long history with the Sikhs, its understanding of the Sikh faith and in no small part because of the indefatigable efforts of many Sikh activists, is much more enlightened on the matter of Sikh identity. Yet, it was with some trepidation that I approached the security checkpoint at the British Parliament in Westminster. It is difficult for me to describe how I felt as I went through security, my Siri Sahib in plain sight, not even eliciting a second glance from the security officers!

As the cast performed at Parliament before a small audience of Members of The House of Lords and The House of Commons, writers, journalists and community members, I found myself reflecting upon the surreal nature of the experience. What had seemed like a pipe dream just a few short months ago, was now reality, because of the efforts of this dedicated group of young actors form Boston and the support of a few visionary individuals who truly understood the potential of the production to touch hearts everywhere!

A lively discussion followed the performance with terrific engagement from the MPs, including Lord Indarjit Singh, one of the Sikh members of the House of Lords. Our host at Parliament, Fabian Hamilton, MP from Leeds North East, was kind enough to give us a quick tour of the Westminster complex before we had to rush to Heathrow to catch our flight back home.

We had one more destination to visit before taking a well-deserved break for Christmas.

We almost did not make it to the San Francisco Bay Area. It had seemed like a terrific destination for Kultar's Mime as the Bay Area was home to a large Sikh community, which included in its ranks some of the best known Sikh entrepreneurs and businessmen in the world as well as many young Sikhs of activist bent. The dates for the Bay Area performances were drawing uncomfortably near when our local coordinator dropped a quiet bombshell by telling me that we had not been able to raise the necessary funding. Several potential Bay Area donors had already contributed to our earlier fundraising efforts, when we were building a war chest to get to India and were reluctant to put more money into the project.

Almost resigned to canceling or rescheduling the performances, I picked up the phone and called my friend Ratinder Paul Singh Ahuja, a successful Silicon Valley entrepreneur, who I had got to know when I was in California seeking stories for my nonfiction work on the Sikh Diaspora in America. Ratinder is easily one of the most interesting Sikhs I have ever met! In addition to being an entrepreneur and philanthropist, Ratinder is also an advanced Tae Known Do master and teacher and a practitioner of the ancient Chinese art of Qi Gong, whose fascinating journey has been documented in the column I write for the Web magazine SikhChic. My hope was that Ratinder would connect me with his network and help me find a handful of supporters who would fund our California trip. Ratinder responded by writing a check to fund the entire trip on his own!

Our Bay Area performances were to be at Stanford and UC Berkeley, they two best known universities in the area. The Stanford performance drew a diverse audience that included several well-known Sikh entrepreneurs. A large contingent form the Sikh Foundation which had supported our efforts to get to India, was led by Dr. Narinder Singh Kapany, the father of Fiber Optics. Dr Kapany and his foundation have done stellar work in many areas supporting and presenting Sikh Art and leading the effort to establish Sikh Studies Chairs at many prestigious universities all over the US. Also in the audience were a few individuals for whom I have a lot of respect. Dr. Ranbir Singh Sandhu is a retired academic who has been a well-respected Sikh activist and thinker for decades. He is one of the most polished, erudite and passionate Sikhs of his generation and has served the community very well as an ambassador in various fora. Mehr and I had earlier spent time with him when we had visited California, documenting stories from the Sikh diaspora.

Our panel after the show was moderated by Jaskaran Kaur, the founder of Ensaaf, a non-profit dedicated to fighting for justice and human rights. Over the years Ensaaf has emerged as a fierce voice in the struggle against oppression with a focus on the Punjab. It was a rare honor for the Kultar's Mime team to share the stage with this young woman, whose struggle for justice truly embodies the ideals that have been the driving force behind the production!

The second Bay Area performance was no less compelling, in great part because of the presence of many students and young people of activist bent, very much in keeping with the heritage of UC Berkeley! Before the performance as I stood in the aisle watching the audience filter in, I was engaged in conversation by two audience members, who seemed rather curious and asked several questions about the Sikh faith and in particular, seemed intrigued by inclusion of lines from Bialik's poem into the play and references to the Kishinev Pogrom, in a work that was clearly focused on the events of 1984 in Delhi. It turned out that both of them were Jewish Studies professors, one from Stanford and the other from UC Berkeley. They had somehow learned about the play and were intrigued enough by its premise and the Jewish connection, to attend. Also in the audience was Eileen Alden whose foray into creating the first Sikh comic book superhero is a hugely interesting story in itself. Later on she told me that her son, who had accompanied her, thought the play 'wasn't bad', which is the closest that one can get to a ringing endorsement from a teen! Needless to say, I am eagerly awaiting the launch of her comic book.

It would be an oversight not to acknowledge an extraordinary young man, Nihal Singh, who attends UC Berkeley and was instrumental in arranging our performance at the University. Nihal, who I first met in the context of Gurmat Sangeet (Sikh Sacred Music) is an excellent musician who has been studying the intricacies of rhythm on the Jori Pakhawaj, the traditional Sikh drum that is employed in Gurmat Sangeet, with Bhai Baldeep Singh. Apart from being a great musician, Nihal is also hands down, one of the brightest young people I have ever met. We have spent many hours in the company of other young musicians reveling in the beauty of Gurmat Sangeet, listening to ancient compositions by the masters and trying to recreate them. When I learned long ago that young Nihal was a staunch conservative, I felt like an uncle whose favorite nephew had contracted a terrible disease, but my affection for him handily trumped my objections to his political leanings that fly in the face of Winston Churchill's much paraphrased aphorism about the connection between the head, the heart, one's age and one's political ideology!

TELLING THE TALE 30 YEARS LATER: THE EXTRAORDINARY JOURNEY OF KULTAR'S MIME PART 6

When Kultar's Mime returned after a break over Christmas, there was a significant change. Michelle, one of the cast members went on to a new project, paving the way for Ross, who had been our Stage Manager until then to step into an acting role. Adelaide Majeski joined the team as our new Stage Manager, as we readied the new cast to resume the tour. Mehr had been away at the National Theater Insititute at the Eugene O'Neill Theater for an intensive one semester program and had been unable to tour with the production until then. Our next few performances were during her winter break, which allowed her to join the next phase of the tour.

Seattle is home to two good friends, Jasmit Singh and Harjinder Singh Sandhu, who were leading the effort to bring the play to the city. I had worked with Jasmit earlier to bring a Gurmat Sangeet (Sikh Sacred Music) event to Seattle several years ago and I remember it being impeccably organized by a large group of very engaged volunteers. The bar, that had already been set high, was handily raised even further! Our Seattle performance was impeccably organized in every way. A late-scheduled Seahawks game ate a bit into our sold-out audience, but it was a smashingly successful resumption of the tour. I was, of course very relaxed as I could leave all the worrying about the show to Mehr and was very happy to schmooze my old college friends Karan Khanna and Monica Goverdhan Kher, from my days at the Birla Institute of Science and Technology, Pilani, who I hadn't seen for thirty years!

We boarded a train the next morning for Portland, the second stop on the tour. Our host in Portland was Pawneet Singh Sethi a dynamic young entrepreneur, who had been a regular visitor to the Gurmat Sangeet Project (a non-profit I founded to preserve and propagate the Sikh Sacred Music Tradition) website for years, unbeknownst to me! Our short time in Portland was packed with many things! The show of course went well, with audience members who in some cases had driven two hours to see the play. After the performance, Mehr and I were interviewed by KBOO, a community radio station in the Portland area.

When we returned to Pawneet's home later, we learned that among other things he was a connoisseur of fine tea. Despite the early start looming the next day, we spent many hours chatting and sampling many different teas from his most impressive collection!

In the audience during our Portland show was regional historian Johanna Ogden, who I had called out of the blue, a couple of years earlier, when I discovered her paper "Ghadar, Historical Silences, and Notions of Belonging *Early 1900s Punjabis of the Columbia River*", published in the Oregon Historical Quarterly. I had then been in California, conducting interviews as part of my research for 'Lions in The West', a nonfiction work documenting the history of the Sikhs in America that I was developing, and it was apparent from Jo's paper that she was likely to be a fount of interesting stories about some of the earliest Sikh immigrants to America.

Jo's research was focused on the city of Astoria in Clatsop County, Oregon. Founded in 1811, with ten thousand people living at the mouth of the Columbia River, it seemed to be just another nondescript American town, with the modest distinction of having been the oldest settlement west of the Rocky Mountains.

I remember having a very cordial conversation with Jo and learning about an upcoming celebration that was to be based on the work that Jo had done, researching the lives of early Punjabi, mostly Sikh immigrants in Astoria. As the he Clatsop County Historical Society's website stated : "Astoria, Oregon will host an October commemoration to mark the 100-year anniversary of the founding of the Ghadar Party, which is considered the beginning of the Indian independence movement. The political movement, driven by Asian Indians, often called "Hindus," of the North American West who wished to free India from British rule, crystallized during a meeting in Astoria's local Finnish Socialist Hall in May 1913."

The most interesting aspect of this celebration was the fact that today in Astoria, there is virtually no trace of these "Hindus", who incidentally, were mostly Sikhs, and their presence in this part of the world. Almost as interesting as the story of the founding of the Ghadar Party, is the modern day tale of how the link between Astoria and the struggle for Indian independence was discovered, by a dogged historian, whose generous embrace of The Other is truly emblematic of what makes this country great.

9-11 was a seminal event that had a profound impact on every American. Some reacted with sorrow; others spewed anger and hate. There were also many, like Johanna Ogden, who turned inwards as the aftermath of 9-11 unfolded, which included the backlash against Muslims and Sikhs, to ponder the question of how, in the flash of an eye, we can start seeing our erstwhile friends and neighbors as The Other, to the extent that we can justify targeting them with violence and death.

From her introspection was born the desire to do something in response. To demonstrate that not everyone in this country felt this way. Several years later, in 2008, as she prepared to enter graduate school, still seeking a specific direction in her personal quest, she crossed paths with Dr. Kambiz Ghanea Bassiri a professor in the Religion Department of Reed College, who was working on a book on the history Islam in America. She credits him with introducing her to the American Punjabi and Sikh community and its role in the Ghadar movement, which she had been unaware of until then.

Jo began researching in Astoria and started finding mentions of deaths and funerals of men with Punjabi names. She kept finding other mention of Punjabis and Sikhs in the papers, in accounts of strikes and wrestling bouts! She learned that many had left Astoria to go fight the British in India. She found census and arrest records. And eventually she found mention of a speech by Ghadar intellectual Har Dyal and a meeting in Astoria's Finnish Socialist Hall in 1913. Tantalizing clues like these led her to suspect that the Punjabi/Sikh community around Astoria had a deep connection to the founding of Gahdar.

Jo struck historical gold after she discovered the work of Harish Puri, a well-known Indian historian, who has done considerable work on the subject and has written several books, documenting his conversations with Ghadarites, decades ago. His work helped her understand the importance of what she was finding. She had found nothing less than the story of Ghadar's emergence and a real sense of how some of the unique features of Astoria at that time contributed to the Ghadar Movement's crystallization! Puri's book had a roadmap, which listed in a few lines, the towns where Ghadar meetings had occurred. The hunt was on! She went to towns all along the Columbia River eventually and tracked down census records as everything was now in focus. The story of the founding of Ghadar in Astoria, would finally be told.

The paper, despite being a scholarly work is readable and highly accessible; although a historian, Jo writes with the sensitivity and the sensibilities of a poet! Jo's compassion for the subjects of her research and the ethos of her work can be clearly felt in the following excerpt :

"The story of Ghadar in the Pacific Northwest is, without a doubt, intriguing. For me, its historical importance lies in the realities it reveals about the transnational making of the region and the historical downplaying, if not silencing, of that very process. The erasure of Asian Indians in Oregon is rooted in myths that have privileged settlement over transience and rigid nationalist fables over stories of global peoples — whether Chinese, Japanese, or Hindustani — who were, and are, intrinsic to the region. Those myths have shaped our archives and stories, and they continue to haunt us through their impact on the notions of belonging and otherness in post-9/11 America. Re-remembering the Punjabis of Oregon — communities of laborers and political activists stretching the length of the Columbia River — prompts one to consider the process of their erasure."

Today, I am delighted to count Jo among my friends. Given her own, generous embrace of 'the other', it was truly wonderful to have her in the audience during our Portland performance.

Our next stop was Washington DC.

We had already presented Kultar's Mime once in collaboration with the Sikh Coalition in New York City, and I had been in discussions with Sapreet Kaur and Rajdeep Singh, the Coalition's attorney in DC about bringing the play to the nation's capital. The Sikh Students Association at The George Washington University, which is located in the heart of DC, was kind enough to arrange the beautiful Dorothy Marvin Betts Theater for us. The performance was well attended with a large student contingent from George Washington University, as well as American University and other area colleges. The Coalition had also sent out invitations to numerous congressional staffers and as a result we had a very diverse audience. Our talkback was moderated by Rubin Paul Singh, also associated with the Sikh Coalition, an extremely articulate and well-spoken young man, who is one of the most promising leaders of his generation.

A second show had been organized at the beautiful Bhai Center in Northern Virginia. Our chief co-conspirator there was Sher Singh, a dear friend of many years with whom I share multiple interests. Sher Singh had the misfortune to achieve national fame in the surreal days that followed 9-11. Sher was based in the DC area in those days but was working with a company in Boston; what happened to him in the aftermath of 9-11 is well worth recounting.

As I drove home from work, the evening of the day that the twin towers were struck, I was listening to NPR. The tragedy was only a few hours old and speculation was rife about the perpetrators. The NPR program was interrupted by a news flash. A young man had been arrested at the Providence Amtrak station on a train bound from Boston to DC. While there was no confirmation that he was involved in the 9-11 plot, the young man had been arrested as a potential terror suspect.

It turned out that that 'terrorist' arrested in Providence was none other than Sher Singh, one of the kindest and gentlest people I know, who was rushing home to DC, driven largely by a desire to do something; anything; any act of service in response to the unspeakable horror that had been unleashed by the terror attack. It so happened that a passenger on the Amtrak train had called in a 'suspicious looking' man who looked Arabic and the authorities saw fit to board the train and search him for daring to look suspicious! An initiated, Amritdhari Singh with a flowing beard, Sher immediately informed the officers that he carried a Kirpan, but to no avail. Perhaps to play to the media circus that had been organized by the then Mayor of Providence, the infamous Buddy Cianci, the officers arrested him with maximum drama, reportedly 'taunting' him by asking 'How's Osama Bin Laden?' and led him away in cuffs in a manner designed to feed the media frenzy that followed.

Right after his arrest several news outlets, most notably Fox News started showing footage of Sher bring led away in handcuffs, juxtaposed with images of Osama Bin Laden in one of the most deplorable acts of stereotyping and fearmongering that I have ever had the misfortune to witness.

Later on that evening after we had learned of the ludicrous arrest, I accompanied several of the leaders of the local Sikh community to Providence. An attorney had been engaged by Sher's family and by then Providence's finest had figured out that the young man was not a terrorist of any stripe! We brought Sher back but the nightmare was far from over. Most news outlets killed the story but Fox news, despite multiple phone calls absolutely refused to pull the footage of a Sikh in handcuffs being arrested after 9-11, overlaid by images of Osama Bin Laden. It is my belief that the frenzy drummed up by Fox News despite knowing that Sikhs had nothing to do with 9-11, played a huge role in inciting the attacks on Sikhs that followed.

Sher's battles were not over either. Buddy Cianci, who was facing a host of investigations, saw it fit to deflect attention from himself by deciding to prosecute Sher for 'carrying a concealed weapon'. At one point a despondent and demoralized Sher was even willing to cop a plea to make the whole mess go away, despite being completely innocent. The local Sikh community, led by Dr. Amritjit Singh, an English professor, rallied and organized multiple protests until sanity prevailed and Sheldon Whitehouse, the then RI Attorney General refused to prosecute the case, finally ending the nightmare.

Sher returned to the DC area and transformed a budding interest in Gurmat Sangeet to found the Guru Angad Academy of Sikh Studies, which thrives today and does an outstanding job connecting young Sikhs to their musical traditions.

Through the efforts of Sher Singh, Rubin Paul Singh, Jasmine Kaur and other friends in the area, the large hall filled up. As the performance began, my thoughts turned from 1984 to the dark days following 9-11. Is it not strange and sad that the veneer of human 'tolerance', 'acceptance' and 'openness' is so terribly thin, even in the so called civilized world.

After we returned from DC, we started to gear up for our second visit to India. But before we got to India, there were three University performances scheduled.

The first one was at Boston University, where the local Sikh Students Association had invited us to perform. Our venue was the gorgeous Alfred L Morse auditorium, built in 1906 as Temple Israel Boston. The building, which was a replica of the Temple of Solomon was a functioning synagogue before the congregation moved and still retains its Jewish character. It was a very appropriate venue for the play, which was well attended by a student audience. The local Gurdwara at Medford had been very kind to arrange for Guru Ka Langar, which was served to all the attendees after the performance and talkback.

Penn State Abington, in the Philadelphia area was our next stop. My good friend Dr. Manohar Singh, who also shares a deep interest in Gurmat Sangeet with me, was our gracious host, as we performed before a very diverse audience that had braved a snowstorm to see the play.

The Sikh Students association of Columbia University, SEWA had been eager to bring the show to the University. On one of the coldest days of the year, we performed at the Roone Arledge Auditorium at Columbia. The audience was dominated by young people, mostly college students, which made for a wonderful talkback. In the audience was Dr. Francesca Cassio, Associate Professor of Music and Sikh Musicology Chair at Hofstra University. Francesca is a wonderful musician, having trained with stalwarts like Ustad Rahim Fahimuddin Dagar and Smt. Girija Devi. She also studied with Bhai Gurcharan Singh, an eleventh generation practitioner of Gurmat Sangeet. Her sensitive and nuanced response to the production greatly enhanced our talkback. Also in the audience was Dr. Balbinder Singh Bhogal, Sikh Studies Chair at Hofstra, who would invite us back to New York for one of our most memorable performances.

TELLING THE TALE 30 YEARS LATER:
THE EXTRAORDINARY JOURNEY OF KULTAR'S
MIME PART 7

It is mid-March in Mumbai. The weather is quite pleasant and the heat hasn't set in yet. Mehr and I find our way to the National Center for the Performing Arts (NCPA) at Nariman Point in downtown Mumbai. The crew has the morning off and is on a tour of the city with local guides, riding the bus, the commuter rail and auto rickshaws as they take in the sights. I have been showing Mehr my old haunts from three decades ago, when as a freshly minted engineer, I worked in the city before leaving for the US to attend graduate school. After a very satisfying lunch at the Britannia Café, one of the storied 'Irani' or Parsi restaurants at Ballard Pier, we go to the NCPA to meet our hosts Mayank and Silky of the Ashima Theater Company.

Mayank and Silky deserve a lot of the credit for making the second Kultar's Mime India tour a reality. Eager to bring the play to non-Sikh audiences in India, I had been casting about for theater connections in various Indian cities. I had been introduced to a few well known theater personalities in Mumbai but the conversations weren't really going anywhere. At that point I decided to search for theater companies online and started cold calling them in an attempt to find a local partner or host in Mumbai. After several lukewarm conversations that went nowhere, I found Mayank, who did show some interest in the play. The handshake occurred a few conversations later and Mayank started scouting around for venues. Later I learned that his chief co-conspirator, Silky was the one who was really intrigued by Kultar's Mime and instrumental in Ashima's decision to partner with us to bring us to Mumbai.

Ashima is a young theater company and bringing a group of US based artists to Mumbai to perform turned out to be a roller coaster ride for them, fraught with red tape, approvals from local censors and unscrupulous touts, who smelt an opportunity to make money, unaware of the frugal, non-profit nature of the production. Ashima doggedly stayed on task and through sheer tenacity, booked two shows at the NCPA, the most prestigious theater venue in Mumbai.

Both performances draw a diverse crowd including several NCPA members who are committed theater buffs. We get written up in local newspapers and Silky does a great job moderating both our talkbacks with aplomb. The reaction of the young non-Sikh audience members is what makes the performances truly memorable for me.

The following quote is from the blog of sixteen year old Tanisha Kamat, who attended the second performance:

I think the fact that the entire cast was New York-based definitely made an even bigger impact because they were people who were in no way connected to India (or even the episode in Russia, for that matter) and couldn't possibly relate to the incidents in the play. And yet, they played their roles to perfection. As it was a movement-based play, they used a lot of gestures and there was a lot of action- including them marching around the audience with torches. They make you feel like you are actually there in the moment and it is all happening once again right before your eyes. They make you feel all the anger, pain, injustice, frustration that the people must have actually felt when those events took place. For this reason, it was a strongly emotional play which had a massive impact on all those watching.

After seeing the way it was depicted, even though it wasn't about my community, I felt so angry and I can't even imagine what it must have been like for all the Sikh people in the audience to relive that moment and yet, at the end, the writer spoke so calmly about how the play did not seek to incite anger or a thirst for revenge in those who watched it. The primary aim of the play was to spread awareness and to get people talking again about events like this which often disappear into oblivion a few months after they have occurred- which is the reason why the play ended with the dialogue "We will never forget."

From Mumbai we fly to Kolkata, once the capital of British India and generally considered to be the birthplace of modern Indian literary and artistic thought. As if it wasn't sufficient to be performing in one of India's richest cultural environments, we have the distinction of being hosted by Padatik, a groundbreaking theater company in Kolkata, where decades ago, Shyamanad Jalan had broken new ground by taking theater out of the proscenium into alternative spaces. Our champion in Kolkata is Anubha Fatehpuria, architect by day and theater artiste by night, who now is the driving force behind Padatik.

Mehr and I can't stop smiling as we step into Padtik's fabulous little performance space. The space has so much character and it looks like it's been created for Kultar's Mime. Our show is sure to look visually fabulous here and it does! The theater staff is absolutely lovely and everyone works hard to make sure that the set is quickly built.

The two Kolkata performances are attended by an erudite audience that includes many artists. Our talkbacks are moderated by Rana Jit, a friend of Anubha's and a filmmaker, who has allowed himself to be drafted. One of the performances is attended by Dr. Ananda Lal, Kolkata's foremost theater critic and an English professor at Jadavpur University. Dr. Lal writes a very generous review of the production in the Telegraph, Kolkata's leading newspaper.

Further delights await us in Kolkata.

On the morning of our second performance, Mehr and I are picked up from our hotel and driven to the home of a man, who I have always held in great esteem. His name is Sardar Saran Singh, who served with distinction in the elite Indian Administrative Service (IAS) for decades before taking over as the editor of the Sikh Review, a highly respected journal, after his retirement. Sardar Saran Singh deserves respect, not only for his accomplishments as a senior bureaucrat and a giant literary figure, but also for his unimpeachable integrity, which gave him the courage to openly and publicly chide Prime Minister Indira Gandhi for her policy blunders in the Punjab, which culminated in the disastrous attack on the Golden Temple in 1984.

Sardar Saran Singh is in his nineties but retains every bit of his legendary graciousness and charm. He welcomes us to his home and hosts us for lunch, presided over by his daughter, Suksham Kaur, who is nothing less than a force of nature herself. Sardar Saran Singh is delighted to learn about Kultar's Mime and he heaps Mehr with encouragement, expressing disappointment at his inability to go to the performance because of his health.

Talk of Kultar's Mime and the dark days following the assassination of Mrs. Gandhi sends Sardar Saran Singh into a reverie and he begins to reminisce. His thoughts take him back to 1983, when he decided to retire after an illustrious career in the IAS, his last posting in Assam as Advisor to the Governor of the State. He talks about his growing alarm at the escalation of the situation in the Punjab and his futile attempts to see the Prime Minister, who knew him well and held him in high esteem, to reason with her and to pull her back from the disastrous inevitability of the policy course that she had set in motion in the Punjab. His attempts to meet her were thwarted by her handlers, several of whom were policy hawks and were salivating at the prospect of reaping the political benefit of a hardline stance in the Punjab that was slowly but surely edging towards violent confrontation.

There is real sadness in his voice as he recounts his failure to stop the events of June 1984 in Amritsar that triggered a cycle of violence that nobody, least of all Mrs. Gandhi could have ever foreseen.

Mehr and I listen. Mesmerized.

The hours fly and it is time for him to rest and we have a performance to put together that night.

The following morning we dash to the airport to catch a flight to Bangalore, the technology capital of India.

Our performance, the same evening in Bangalore, is at Jagriti, one of the city's most prestigious theater venues, managed by Arundhati and

Jagdish Raja, founders of the Artists Repertory Theater. Our Bangalore performance has been arranged through the efforts of Nimmi Sankaran, an old friend, who runs the education startup, Hey Math. The Bangalore performance is on a weeknight and traffic in the city has always been terrible. It is time for the doors to open and the foyer is teeming. The audience includes many avid theater goers, who are Jagriti regulars. Jagdigh Raja, extremely urbane and well read, does an outstanding job moderating the panel during the talkback.

From Bangalore, we dash to Chennai the next morning. Chennai is a city that I have strong ties to. During a previous life after being bitten by the entrepreneurial bug, I had quit the US tech behemoth that I then worked for to work for a small software company based in Chennai called Futuresoft. Over the next two years, I spent a lot of time in the city as I helped reengineer the company and position it for growth, leading to its eventual acquisition. I developed many friendships and had some very fond memories of the city. The Chennai performance had been organized by a friend from my days as an undergraduate at BITS, Pilani, Ravin Kurian, who had been following the fortunes of Kultar's Mime on Facebook and had offered to help bring the production to Chennai.

Our host in Chennai is Sadanand Menon, a well-known journalist, arts editor, teacher of cultural journalism, photographer, stage lights designer and frequent speaker at seminars on politics, ecology and the arts. Sadanand has been a close associate of the legendary choreographer and dancer, Chandralekha and he has graciously offered us a beautiful venue called Spaces that had been conceived by her, which he now oversees. Sadanand Menon, as it turns out, has a strong connection to the events that unfolded in Delhi in October 1984. Quite by chance, he happened to be in Delhi when Mrs. Gandhi was assassinated. He proceeded to take many photographs of the carnage, which were commandeered by various inquiry commissions into the violence that had been seated in the thirty years that had passed. Unfortunately, none of his photographs were ever returned to him.

Sadanand welcomes us to Spaces, which is a serenely beautiful venue on the outskirts of Chennai, right on the ocean in Basant Nagar. It is an open air theater, surrounded by palm trees and foliage with a sand floor. As we prepare for the performance, a soft ocean breeze blowing, I feel almost like I felt in Preet Nagar, as my imagination conjured up the spirits of artists and their muses past. Sadanand Menon is a warm and wonderful presence who makes us feel very welcome.

We are far from the city and it is Thursday evening. I am convinced that our audience will consist of Ravin, Sadanand and perhaps a half a dozen of their close friends! As night falls and the breeze becomes stronger, a crowd begins to form in the foyer. I see some familiar faces but there is a sea of humanity out there, waiting to be seated. Spaces is completely full! There is not even any standing room left. Tonight's performance is one of our most memorable. Perhaps the cast is inspired too, by the unexpectedly large audience and the spirits that inhabit this beautiful place.

Some of my heroes are in the audience today.

Teesta Setalvad is a well-known Indian Civil Rights activist and journalist. She runs the Citizens for Justice and Peace, an organization she created to fight for justice for the victims of sectarian violence in Gujrat in 2002. She and her husband, Javed Anand, a journalist and activist have been constantly harried and harassed by powerful politicians in India, who have a vested interest in blocking their quest for justice and transparency. It is an honor for the Kultar's Mime team to have Teesta Setalvad and Javed Anand in the audience today. During the talkback, following the performance, I sit back and listen to her speak. At other talkbacks, I have often made the point that the stories of all the innocent victims of sectarian violence are connected. Today her presence makes that connection palpable.

The moderator of our talkback is Sashi Kumar. Several years ago, just as my involvement with Futresoft was winding down, I remember reading a story about a film on 1984, called Kaya Taran, which had been made by a Chennai based filmmaker, tucked away in an obscure corner in one of the Chennai papers. The subject of the film immediately piqued my interest. Based on a short story called 'When Big Trees Fall' by N.S.Madhavan, it told the story of a young Sikh mother and her child, who seek refuge in a hospice for dying nuns in the provincial town on Meerut, fleeing a bloodthirsty mob that has attacked and killed the rest of their family. The film, by virtue of its subject matter, was never going to be a Bollywood blockbuster and sure enough it faded into obscurity despite winning the prestigious Aravindan Award. I had been able to acquire a DVD of the film thorough the efforts of one of my Chennai lieutenants and was completely blown away by the sensitivity with which the subject of the 1984 violence had been handled. Kaya Taran is a fabulous film and truly deserves to be seen widely. It was one of the works of art that the Kultar's Mime cast engaged with during their dramaturgical work and it is not an exaggeration to say that their work on the play has been informed by this extraordinary film.

The filmmaker was none other than Sashi Kumar, who is well known for having stared Asianet, one of India's first regional satellite channels and founding the Asian College of Journalism. When Ravin had first connected me to Sadanand Menon, I had asked him if he knew Sashi Kumar and learned that he knew him extremely well, which should not have come as a surprise, given the prominent place that they both occupy in the Chennai arts scene. I asked for an introduction and proceeded to invite him to the Kultar's Mime performance in Chennai. Emboldened by his ready acceptance, I asked him to moderate our panel after the performance and I was absolutely thrilled when he agreed.

It is such a treat to have Sashi Kumar as our moderator. His own sensitive engagement with 1984 informs his introductory remarks. The conversation with the audience is wide ranging, embracing subjects as broad as the causes of the violence and very technical theatrical aspects of the play. An elderly gentleman even attempts to somehow blame the Sikhs for being attacked in 1984, suggesting they 'brought it upon themselves' by emphasizing their separateness from the Hindu fold, a specious argument that I politely but firmly debunk to resounding applause from the overwhelmingly non-Sikh audience.

My mind is in a whirl. Here I am, in Chennai, far from the Sikh homeland the Punjab, talking about the pain of the Sikhs. With me is a brilliant filmmaker who has beautifully told a story that epitomizes 'embracing the pain of the other', which is a theme writ large on Kultar's Mime. A few feet from us sits a Hindu woman, who has bravely set out on a quest to seek justice for the Muslim minority of Gujarat, which was set upon and victimized in the 2002 carnage. All of a sudden, for a wonderful moment, everything that Kultar's Mime has tried to accomplish through this journey becomes very real. I feel a rush of exhilaration, compassion and humility, all at once.

I cannot leave Chennai without acknowledging the ghost of Chandralekha, for she is our true host tonight. We sit in the beautiful and serene place that she created. Surely she is here too, looking down benignly upon us. My thoughts drift to Kaya Taran again.

One of the most powerful moments in the film is a stylized dance, eerie in conception, executed brilliantly by Navtej Johar, the well-known Sikh exponent of Bharat Natyam, an ancient Southern Indian dance form, with a group of female dancers. The dance has stayed in my mind ever since I first saw the film a decade ago. It is beautiful, yet very disturbing and it comes at one of the most traumatic moments in the film. It is surreal.

It turns out that the dance was choreographed by none other than Chandralekha!

Delhi beckons and we leave early the next morning. Our first performance is to be at Kamani Hall, one of Delhi's most prestigious theater venues, as part of the Atelier Campus Theatre festival, organized by none other than my friend Prof. Kuljeet Singh. Our second performance will take us back to Akshara Theater, where six months ago, we had first presented Kultar's Mime in Delhi, our hearts in our mouths! This performance is going to be special as our co-host is none other than HS Phoolka the indefatigable crusader for the rights of the victims of 1984. He has invited many of Delhi's political elites and in particular we are expecting a galaxy of civil rights activists. The upstart populists of the Aam Aadmi Party will be well represented as well the Lokraj Sangathan. Several leaders of the Bachpan Bachao Andolan, a nonprofit run by the recently anointed Nobel Laureate, Kailash Satyarthi will be present as well. I am most excited because Gopal Sharman, the founder of Akshara and his wife Jalabala Vaidya, a groundbreaking theater artist who performed the Ramayana on Broadway in the 1960s will be in attendance. Mr. Phoolka has just informed me that the well-known artist, Arpana Cour, whose work I am a great admirer of, also plans to attend.

We leave for Delhi with a sense of anticipation. Our last few days with Kultar's Mime in India are bound to be memorable!

TELLING THE TALE 30 YEARS LATER: THE EXTRAORDINARY JOURNEY OF KULTAR'S MIME PART 8

What is it that I hope to find?

> *In these dusty alleys; forbidden; unkind*

My own words, written more than twenty-five years ago, haunt me as Mehr and I walk the narrow and filthy streets of Tilakvihar, also known as The Widow Colony.

The tale has been told thirty-four times already. They have all listened rapt. The mighty and the weak. The famous and the anonymous. Scholars and illiterates. Rich and poor. Most with writhing hearts and salty cheeks. Why? Because at the end of the day, this could be anyone's story. Many a time have they asked. 'Did you go *there*'?. 'Did you meet *them*'?

Our answer until now also always been a shake of the head, followed by a torrent of words, explaining why. We don't want to be disrespectful of the victims. We don't want to reopen their wounds. We don't want to exploit their pain, which is ever present, unending, in any way.

But the pull of Tilakvihar is too strong. We can't stay away and yet I am at a loss to find the right way to do it.

Once again, Dr. Uma Chakravarti comes to the rescue.

A few weeks earlier, on the phone leading up to the second India tour of Kultar's Mime, Dr. Charkravarti had said something that felt not un- like a stinging slap on my face. 'You Sikhs have abandoned the survivors of 1984', were her exact words, delivered in her trademark straightforward manner. Flushed with the recent success of Kultar's Mime, I remember feeling a little indignant, before acknowledging that as much as Kultar's Mime had helped restart the conversation about 1984, it was quite irrel- evant to the survivors who continue to scratch out a miserable existence in Tilakvihar.

Dr. Chakravarti told a desolate tale of three generations; the first devastated by the horrific violence, the second by drugs and alcohol as hundreds of young men grew up with no authority figures or male role models in their lives as their widowed, mostly illiterate mothers were singularly focused on providing for the tattered remnants of their families. The third generation, she said was now in jeopardy as nothing of note had been done in the thirty years that had passed since the carnage.

She encouraged me to go to Tilakvihar and to see for myself and she offered to introduce me to social workers and human rights activists, who had won the survivors' trust by tirelessly working with them as they struggled to survive.

This is how Mehr and I end up walking the inhospitable and miserable streets of Tilakvihar. And miserable they are! More miserable than I had ever imagined them to be! Everywhere are the unmistakable signs of poverty and neglect. Crumbling buildings. Peeling paint. Piles of refuse everywhere. Narrow alleys piled with rubble. Our guide is Amar Nijhawan, a young Canadian woman and recent college graduate, who has chosen to serve the survivors of Tilakvihar, working with a non-profit called Aman Biradari. It is a busy day for Amar; the next day a community center for the survivors is being inaugurated and she has brought with her a young artist who will paint murals on the walls of the room that will serve as a library in the community center.

We briefly look into the new library, which is a tiny room in a ground floor apartment, its walls painted in bright colors. We pass clusters of young girls with their hair in plaits. They break into shy smiles when they see Amar and some of them run up to her to hug her. We climb several flights of stairs to enter a tiny apartment, which is Baby Kaur's world. Baby Kaur is a short, light skinned woman, probably in her mid to early forties. She greets us cordially and invites us to sit in her in her tiny parlor. Mehr looks a little nonplussed when she is offered water but I politely and somewhat embarrassedly decline on everyone's behalf. Amar briefly explains that we only drink bottled water as we are from 'abroad'. Already uncomfortable at our imposition, I feel terrible having to refuse the water; at suggesting to Baby Kaur that her water is not good enough for us to drink, but she takes it in stride and does not appear offended.

How do you talk to a survivor of something as horrible as 1984? You struggle for an opening as you try to find something meaningful to say. Something compassionate. Something humanizing. Something that won't make your interest seem superficial , or even worse, voyeuristic. Somehow we stumble into those dark days thirty years ago and Baby Kaur's narrative slowly emerges, almost of its own accord. It is of course heart wrenching. As horrifying as her recollections of 1984 is her story of the struggle to survive as a poor, neglected and orphaned teen, desperately trying to hold her family together as one set of vague promises of help and rehabilitation fades, yielding to others equally lacking in substance.

The tears are lurking somewhere very close beneath her calm and cheerful exterior and they emerge of their own accord as she relives the horrors of the last thirty years. As I commiserate with her, I want to share with her the love and compassion of thousands of strangers from all around the world, who have wept upon embracing the stories of Baby Kaur and her siblings in sorrow. I find myself talking about the play and its journey in an attempt to convey some of that to her and then very hesitatingly, I find myself asking if she by any chance knows a young man called Avatar, who would probably be in his mid-thirties; who was deaf and mute; who had suffered the terrible pain of watching his father being lynched before his own eyes.

I am dumbfounded when she says yes!

I must confess that the thought has been in the back of my mind but I am not quite sure of how to process the fact that this young man, who was until this moment a character in a story, is alive and present and indeed nearby. I am of course happy and yet 3at the same time inexplicably fearful. How will he take it, when he learns that his pain has been shared with thousands of strangers? Will this knowledge rip the scabs off wounds that are not quite healed? For an instant the Kultar's Mime journey becomes an impossibly heavy burden that crushes me but after a small silence I ask if we can visit him.

Baby Kaur explains that he lives nearby but is most likely at work; he is one of the fortunate few in the colony who have a 'government job'. We are terribly disappointed because we know that we will not have time to return to Tilakvihar and on a whim, I ask Baby Kaur if we can visit his home at least, even if there is a very slim chance of finding him there.

Baby Kaur and Seema Kaur, another survivor, lead our little procession through the alleyways of Tilakvihar. We pass a small park, desolate and overrun with trash where a ragtag band of little street urchins is gathered, looking at us with great curiosity. Hardly a unique sight in a poor Delhi neighborhood, with the exception that all of the boys are Sikh. They wear ragged clothes and most of the sport joodas (top knots) on their heads. A young Sikh, in his mid-twenties, sits in their midst. As I walk up to the little band, all of them rise to their feet and greet me with shy smiles. These are the grandchildren of Tilakvihar; the third generation of survivors. The young man tells me that he is a volunteer, who teaches the children Punjabi.

As we walk through the trash filled streets, I find many conflicting emotions coursing through me. There is nothing in Tilakvihar to feel good about. It is a sad, miserable place suffused with the pain of the survivors, whose palpable grief hangs like a pall upon its shattered neighborhoods. The shy smiles of the young children who greet us are a testimonial to the resiliency of human life, but I cannot help despairing at the bleak existence that almost inevitably seems to be their future, bereft as they are of resources and support, thirty years after the unspeakable calamity that turned the lives of their families upside down.

And yet, as I look into the eyes of the young Punjabi teacher, I see not despair, but a quiet determination. Amar Nijhawan walks ahead of me, her shoulders straight; unbowed by the burden that she has chosen to carry willingly and cheerfully.

After walking for what seems like forever, assailed by the misery of Tilakvihar, we climb a narrow flight of stairs to an apartment block that is indistinguishable from its neighbors. We are at Avatar's apartment and a heavy lock swings from the door.

Deeply disappointed, we head back to the street, but the ever resourceful Baby Kaur, who has decided to knock on neighboring doors, excitedly beckons, asking us to return. In the landing stands a young woman, carrying an infant, an older child in tow, looking somewhat suspiciously at our little group.

Seema Kaur talks to her rapidly in a language that sounds quite unfamiliar and she opens the door, inviting us into her parlor, which is as tiny as Baby Kaur's. All of us squeeze in, accompanied by a few curious neighbors and an assortment of children.

The woman's name is Gurmeet Kaur. She is from Rajasthan and is of Sindhi origin. She has been married to Avatar for eight years. She pulls out a smartphone and starts texting.

A few minutes later, a very handsome young man in his mid-thirties stands at the door, perhaps a bit nonplussed at the sight of so many strangers crowded into his little parlor. Everyone starts talking all at once and I learn about the journey of the child who used his little body to tell the heartbreaking tale of his father's brutal murder.

Like many other survivors of Trilokpuri and other 'Trans Yamuna' neighborhoods where the worst carnage took place, the shattered remnants of Avatar's family were brought to Tilakvihar to be 'resettled'. Each family was given a tiny one room apartment and was promised a coveted government job, which would give them some form of subsistence. Avatar was one of the lucky ones, as his mother was given a job at the Tihar Prison in Delhi. It was probably a miracle wrought by the character of his late mother, that this young boy, who suffered such unspeakable trauma in 1984, grew up in Tilakvihar avoiding the ever present lure of drugs and alcohol, that most of his peers succumbed to.

As I learn of the impossible story of how Avatar survived and thrived, I feel the burden lifting. This young man, against all odds, living in the desolate confines of Tilakvihar, has impossibly carved out a life for himself. A life that includes a wife, who is clearly proud of his accomplishments, two beautiful children, a job and a home. It is also remarkable that through all this he has stayed connected to his faith and his identity.

The faith of the Sikhs of Delhi has been tested many times. As I look at this proud young Sikh in his impeccably wound turban, my thoughts drift back to the time, almost three hundred and fifty years ago, when the Sikhs of Delhi were devastated by the execution of Gur Tegh Bahadur Sahib, the ninth Sikh Guru. The Guru's body and severed head lying unclaimed in Chandni Chowk (one of Delhi's best known streets), I am sure, must have forced many Sikhs to reexamine their personal commitment to their faith and its consequences. In the dark days of 1984, many Sikhs in Delhi were similarly forced to reflect upon the implications of being a Sikh. It is impossible for me to put myself in the shoes of someone who saw their entire life go up in flames and it is absolutely unconscionable to judge any Sikh who made the difficult choice of effacing his very visible identity in the face of such savagery. It is a well-known fact that many did! Yet, I cannot help but feel tremendous admiration for this young man, who could have slipped into despair. Who could have sought the embrace of drugs or alcohol to blunt his pain, as many of his peers did. Who could have shed the identity which had brought him and his family so much suffering.

But he didn't.

The story of Avatar's survival is almost miraculous in itself. The story of his surviving and thriving with his identity intact is heroic. It is a slap on the face of every bigot and every tyrant who has attempted to do harm to someone else, driven by pure hatred. For Avatar is not alone. Just as he has survived and thrived there are millions, all over the world who continue to rise, phoenix like, from the ashes of destruction wrought by hatred, affirming with their resilience that no matter how difficult the circumstances, the human spirit will endure. This is what gives me hope, no matter how many fires continue to burn all over the world.

Gurmeet Kaur, Avatar's wife has an animated conversation in sign language with her husband. She is telling him about our journey; where his story has been and the countless strangers who send him their love and goodwill. He glances at me and Mehr several times, nodding and when she is done, he reaches for a pen and scribbles on his hand. His outstretched palm, which he holds up for us to see, simply says: 'Thank You!'.

ACKNOWLEDGEMENTS

There are many to thank for the tremendous success of Kultar's Mime.

Gobinda Mukhoty, former President, PUDR and Rajni Kothari, former President, PUCL took a principled and courageous stand by publishing 'Who Are The Guilty ?' which unflinchingly told the true story of the 1984 Delhi massacre. Similarly, Madhu Kishwar, in sharp contrast to the most of the Indian press, fearlessly reported what was really happening in Delhi during the massacre. Dr. Veena Das very poignantly captured the pain of the Sikh children who survived the massacre in her research work. Kultar's Mime owes its existence to the integrity and courage of these extraordinary individuals.

Harinder Singh, formerly of the Sikh Research Institute had the vision to provide a platform for reviving Kultar's Mime. We are indebted to the Sikh Research Institute for initially funding and nurturing the production of Kultar's Mime, which continues to tell the story of the massacre around the world.

T.Sher Singh, pioneering Canadian Sikh attorney and the editor of SikhChic has been a supporter of this project since its inception. His encouragement and broad vision greatly inspired us to be ambitious and believe in our ability to restart the conversation about 1984. Dr. Uma Chakravarti, academic and one of India's best known feminists, very quickly became a mentor to Kultar's Mime and provided not just encouragement but also a deep connection to the survivors of 1984, who have been the recipients of her compassionate support for thirty years. Professor Kuljit Singh of Atelier Expressions was instrumental in bringing the production to Delhi on the 30th anniversary of the massacre. After that, there was simply no turning back!

Several individuals were instrumental in enabling us to travel the world, telling the story of 1984, through their generous support of the project. These include Ratinder Paul Singh Ahuja, Amarpreet & Deepika Sawhney, Farhad & Flora Khosravi, The Chardi Kala Foundation, The Sikh Foundation, Amandeep & Manpreet Khurana, Mayank Bawa & Amrit Kaur Sethi, Jassi & Preeti Chadha, Dr. Kulvinderjit Singh, Gurparkash Singh & Satbir Kaur, S. Mandair, Anup & Nikki Khatra & Ravijit Paintal.

As the Kultar's Mime team has traveled through The US, Canada, England, Scotland and India, we have experienced the warmth and hospitality of many individuals, who have hosted us, fed us, driven us around, arranged our performances and treated us as if we were part of their families. Your warmth and affection will always be remembered by each and every member of the Kultar's Mime team.

Finally, we would like to thank S. Gurdip Singh Malik for his generous support which made the publication of Kultar's Mime possible.

J.Mehr Kaur & Sarbpreet Singh

Made in the USA
Middletown, DE
02 November 2023

41777159R00116